Inside Disney

the
Incredible Story of
Walt Disney
World
and the Man
Behind the Mouse

2nd Edition

Other Unofficial Guides

Beyond Disney: The Unofficial Guide to Universal, SeaWorld, and the Best of Central Florida

Mini Las Vegas: The Pocket-Sized Unofficial Guide to Las Vegas

Mini-Mickey: The Pocket-Sized Unofficial Guide to Walt Disney World

The Unofficial Guides to Bed & Breakfasts and Country Inns: California Great Lakes States Mid-Atlantic New England Northwest Rockies Southeast Southwest

The Unofficial Guides to the Best RV and Tent Campgrounds: California & the West Florida & the Southeast Great Lakes Mid-Atlantic States Northeast Northwest Southwest U.S.A.

The Unofficial Guide to Branson, Missouri

The Unofficial Guide to Chicago

The Unofficial Guide to Cruises

The Unofficial Guide to Disneyland

The Unofficial Guide to Disneyland Paris

The Unofficial Guide to Florence, Rome, and the Heart of Italy

The Unofficial Guide to the Great Smoky and Blue Ridge Region

The Unofficial Guide to Golf Vacations in the Eastern U.S.

The Unofficial Guide to Hawaii

The Unofficial Guide to Las Vegas

The Unofficial Guide to London

The Unofficial Guide to New Orleans

The Unofficial Guide to New York City

The Unofficial Guide to Paris

The Unofficial Guide to San Francisco

The Unofficial Guide to South Florida, including Miami and the Keys

The Unofficial Guides to Traveling with Kids: California Florida Mid-Atlantic New England and New York Walt Disney World

The Unofficial Guide to Walt Disney World

The Unofficial Guide to Walt Disney World for Grown-Ups

The Unofficial Guide to Washington, D.C.

The Unofficial Guide to the World's Best Diving Vacations

Inside Disney

the
Incredible Story of
Walt Disney
World
and the Man
Behind the Mouse

2nd Edition

Eve Zibart

Wiley Publishing, Inc.

Please note that prices fluctuate in the course of time, and travel information changes under the impact of many factors that influence the travel industry. We therefore suggest that you write or call ahead for confirmation when making your travel plans. Every effort has been made to ensure the accuracy of information throughout this book, and the contents of this publication are believed correct at the time of printing. Nevertheless, the publishers cannot accept responsibility for errors or omissions or for changes in details given in this guide or for the consequences of any reliance on the information provided by the same. Assessments of attractions and so forth are based upon the author's own experience, and therefore, descriptions given in this guide necessarily contain an element of subjective opinion, which may not reflect the publisher's opinion or dictate a reader's own experience on another occasion. Readers are invited to write the publisher with ideas, comments, and suggestions for future editions.

Published by:

Wiley Publishing, Inc.
909 Third Avenue
New York, NY 10022

Produced by Menasha Ridge Press
COVER DESIGN BY MICHAEL J. FREELAND
INTERIOR DESIGN BY MICHELE LASEAU

For information on our other products and services or to obtain technical support, please contact our Customer Care Department within the U.S. at (800) 762-2974, outside the U.S. at (317) 572-3993, or fax (317) 572-4002

Wiley also publishes its books in a variety of electronic formats. Some content that appears in print may not be available in electronic formats.

ISBN 0-7645-6443-9

ISSN 1524-8534

Manufactured in the United States of America

Contents

Animal, Vegetable, or Mineral?

Mickey & Company

Afterword

Appendix

Acknowledgments

This book would not have been possible without the assistance of many sources, both on and off the record, and on and off the Internet. My gratitude.

I am especially grateful for the professional courtesy of the *Orlando Sentinel,* the newspaper that made Walt Disney World possible in the first place. The *Sentinel* has striven ever since to make sure the company lived up to its promises. Its archives were invaluable.

Thanks as always to the folks at Menasha Ridge Press, especially Bob, Molly, Holly, Patt, and Mary Ellen.

My warmest thanks, however, go to Heather Freeman, who not only opened her home to me as a base of operations and tolerated my stress jags and long hours (and covered me with comforting animals), but who gave me reason to remember that the most magical kingdom is the one your friends' affection constructs around you. This book is for her.

—*With love, Eve*

Preface

Welcome to the World

The night before Walt Disney died, he called his chief of operations, Admiral Joe Fowler, to the hospital. Lying in his bed, Disney pointed to the ceiling, and on that blank white "sheet" he drew his dream park's layout, its shape, its flow. "As ill as he was," Fowler told the *Orlando Sentinel* more than 20 years later, "he acted like a boy just let out of school. The last draft of what is now Disney World was sketched out, figuratively, on that ceiling. And the next day, he died."

Most castles in the air are never built. But Walt Disney's was, and it became the symbol of one of the most successful corporate kingdoms ever created—one worth an estimated $90 billion at one time. But it wasn't always the park Walt envisioned, and its "last draft" is far from finished.

This is not a tour guide to Walt Disney World; it does not replicate *The Unofficial Guide to Walt Disney World,* its companion volume that evaluates every ride and tells you how to get the most out of your time at the park. It is neither exposé nor promotional brochure. Instead, this is a book for the armchair traveler, the repeat customer, or the trivia fan—a reader's companion to the largest, most opulent, fascinating, and vital theme park in history.

This is a different kind of stroll through Disney World: part history, part myth, part whodunit and how. It's a mixture of intuition, interpretation, and investigation. It's a look at the nuts-and-bolts of a few rides (everything but the whirl), the amazing facts and fictions of the landscaping (the roots of the problems), the grown-ups' attractions and bars (Is there a new sort of "mickey" in the works?), and a few real-life hazards (what

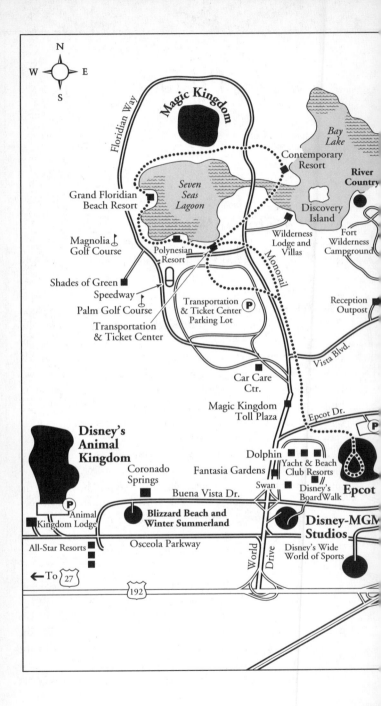

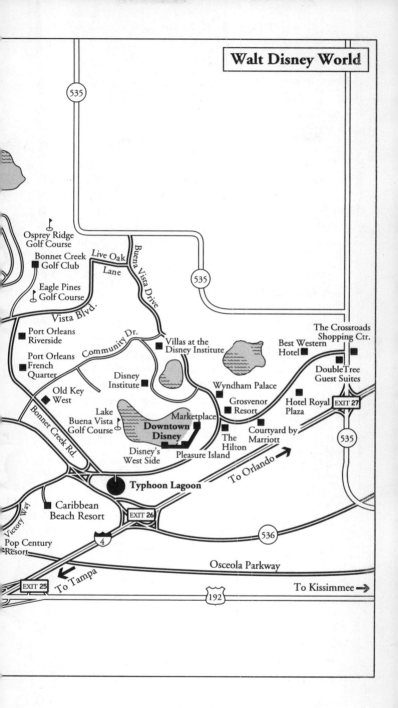

535

Osprey Ridge
Golf Course

Bonnet Creek
Golf Club

Live Oak
Lane

Buena Vista Drive

535

Eagle Pines
Golf Course

Vista Blvd.

The Crossroads
Shopping Ctr.

Port Orleans
Riverside

Community Dr.

Villas at the
Disney Institute

Best Western
Hotel

DoubleTree
Guest Suites

Port Orleans
French
Quarter

Disney
Institute

Wyndham Palace

Hotel Royal
Plaza

EXIT 27

Old Key
West

Grosvenor
Resort

535

Lake
Buena Vista
Golf Course

Marketplace

**Downtown
Disney**

Courtyard by
Marriott

Bonnet Creek Rd.

Disney's
West Side

The
Hilton

Pleasure Island

To Orlando

Typhoon Lagoon

Victory Way

Caribbean
Beach Resort

EXIT 26

To Tampa

Pop Century
Resort

4

536

EXIT 25

Osceola Parkway

192

To Kissimmee →

it's like to be the mouse behind the mask). It's not the final word on the park—that may never be written, considering how many new hotels and attractions are constantly being constructed—but it should answer some of your questions and give you something to pass the time while you're standing in line for Space Mountain.

As Disney itself has reminded us, Beauty is in the eye of the beholder—and so is the Beast. So in this book, we mix kudos and carping. We raise some cultural qualms about the treatment of women, blacks, and other minorities in the park's attractions, but we also applaud some of the policies toward minority employees of the company. We shake off some of the "pixie dust," perhaps, but the business savvy and the scientific and technological glitter are far more impressive—and so are some of the shortcuts, in their own way.

And we consider "the kingdom's" two rulers: Walt Disney himself and crown prince Michael Eisner, at once Walt's opposite and his natural heir. The building, and the rebuilding, of Walt Disney World and the Disney Company is a Hollywood story in its own right, full of intrigue, dummy companies, gigantic budgets, family squabbles, Wall Street jitters, and record-breaking grosses.

And we can't forget the magic, of course. After all, "magic" is the kingdom's middle name.

Introduction

A View of the World

The story goes that author Ray Bradbury, himself a fairly sophisticated prognosticator of socioscientific advances, was so dazzled by the original Disneyland that he asked Walt Disney to consider running for mayor of Los Angeles. After a moment's thought, Disney supposedly responded, "Why should I run for mayor when I'm already king?"

The Magic Kingdom may have been Walt's crowning achievement. But Walt Disney World, the house the Mouse built, is far more influential now, a whole generation after its opening, than Walt could ever have dreamed. Walt Disney World has not only transformed the entertainment industry, but has pushed the envelopes of visual and electronic effects, psychological packaging, merchandising, and land management—and has put a serious dent into the nation's impression of its own history.

The theme parks that most people see are only a fraction of the whole World, not only in the physical sense (the Magic Kingdom alone has nine acres of "basement"), but financially, politically, technologically, and sociologically. It is a fascinating amalgam of capitalism, free enterprise, socialism, artistic patronage, "green" politics, and rigid, one might almost say "Red," employee rules.

When it comes to talking money, Disney dollars are metaphorical gold. The phrase "hundreds of millions" scarcely even applies anymore. The company has spent approximately $15 billion on sports acquisitions, franchise bids, broadcast regions, and facilities over the last five or six years. More than a billion dollars' worth of new hotels and attractions are in some stage of construction at almost any time. Celebration, the model town of

20,000 residents that Disney built in Osceola County, cost $2.5 billion. But even that pales in comparison to the $19.5-billion deal Disney made in August 1995 to purchase the Capital Cities/ABC television network company.

Billions in, billions out. The value of Disney stock increased 27% a year during Eisner's first 13 years as CEO, and its market capitalization climbed from less than $2 billion in 1984 to $90 billion in 2000. And even with its much-publicized troubles of recent years, most financial observers believe Eisner has turned the company around again, and several key investment gurus have recommended buying the stock before it balloons once more. For more on Disney's financial doings, see the chapter "The Mouse That Scored: The Michael Eisner Era."

Walt Disney World is its own city-state: officially, the Reedy Creek Improvement District, an entity as self-sufficient as its predecessors of the Italian Renaissance, and bigger than some. (Some Florida officials have referred to it as "the Vatican.") It has its own taxing authority and the power to issue bonds. It makes its own zoning decisions and sets its own building codes, which are actually stricter than those of most other American cities. It supplies and maintains all the power for Walt Disney World, producing about 25% of it within the Reedy Creek District itself and buying the rest. It has its own Environmental Protection Department. It issues its own building permits, and its bottom-line attitude toward labor and construction has allowed the company repeatedly to meet what seemed to be impossibly short deadlines. The taxes it levies pay for utilities, roads and infrastructure, fire protection, and public transportation within the district; the taxes it pays Osceola and Orange Counties (the Disney tract straddles both) go for police, education, and welfare services.

The company's progressive—or pre-emptive, depending on your viewpoint—dealings with labor unions is the envy of other municipalities. In 1969, during the construction of Walt Disney World, a three-year agreement involving Disney and the AFL-CIO promised that in the case of contractual disagreements, a neutral umpire would be called in within 24 hours to issue an immediate decision if the local unions agreed not to strike, picket, or stop work until the project was complete. And to make sure the project was overseen by someone with hands-on experience, Disney hired Major General William Everett "Joe" Potter, an MIT-trained Army chief engineer, former governor of the Panama Canal Zone, and second-in-command of the New York World's Fair.

The internal structure of the park and its attractions are the envy of urban planners as well. Most of Walt Disney World has been designed by artists and engineers called "Imagineers," who create the attractions from inside out—that is, starting with the show, then sketching the theater, and then the architecture itself—rather than always beginning with square footage and configuration. Disney engineers developed an innovative system of water reclamation to prevent either flooding or excessive drainage—continual threats in the central Florida wetlands—and Disney World was the first U. S. property to install a fully automated vacuuming and compacting trash collection system that uses pneumatic tubes.

Its telecommunications company, a joint venture of Disney and United Telecommunications, produced the first fully electronic telephone system (with all underground cable), the first commercial fiber-optic system for voice in the country, and one of the first computer-controlled systems. In 1985, it became the first telephone company to go completely digital. Disney World has a satellite system/cable TV network; a private "red line" satellite hook-up to Walt Disney Productions in California; and an interactive audio/video information system throughout Epcot that provides directions, background, routes, and updated schedules for the entire park. Engineers are currently working on a hand-held captioning device that would allow hearing-disabled visitors a real-time experience in situations where interpreters or listening devices are inappropriate or insufficient.

But it isn't just the technology or politics of Walt Disney World that make it interesting; it's the World's role in our world, its peculiar and frankly prettied-up view of American culture. Anthropologist Stephen M. Fjellman, in his landmark and somewhat rococo study, *Vinyl Leaves: Walt Disney World and America,* takes a sort of modified Marshall McLuhan approach to Walt Disney World: the medium is the message is the marketing.

Fjellman is concerned that we recognize Walt Disney World as a "commodity," a product prepared for mass consumption, and he wants visitors to be aware of the underlying messages—in some cases, biases—being perpetrated by certain attractions. Fjellman calls it "the most ideologically important piece of land in the United States . . . the quintessence of the American way," because it has not only perfected the balance of nostalgia and personal accommodation, but has assembled a huge network of media tie-ins, button-pushing hype, and marketing savvy to make sure the nostalgia continues to sell.

Fjellman says that Walt Disney World has captured "the symbolic essence of childhood" as opposed, presumably, to an actual experience. It combines memories from images either seen in fact or "borrowed" from cultural artifacts (just the sort of bowdlerized nostalgia that permeated Disney movies in the old days as well). He points out that much of the experience is physically passive—he sees the overall structure as cinematic, a "you are there" in 3-D—and that most of our responses are not only carefully orchestrated but built into the actual design in terms of timing of special effects and so on.

He also points out that in its immaculate cleanliness, its strict-to-the-script casting, its crime-free and car-free Main Street, and its almost religious anti-littering and anti-pollution design, Disney World provides an *apparent* antidote to the fears, the increasing isolationism, and the professional/personal fracturing of everyday life. It is a sort of Oz at the heart of Kansas, he says, and like all Ozes, it has a would-be wizard (in this case, hundreds of them) pulling strings behind the curtain. Where most of us see Cinderella Castle, Fjellman sees Fritz Lang's *Metropolis,* the luxury above coming at the expense of the utility corridors and concession carts and service workers laboring underground.

Unlike a lot of Walt Disney World critics, Fjellman has spent a great deal of time at the park and is genuinely fond of it despite the valid questions it raises. Other observers have raised similarly valid criticisms, including the fact that over a period of years, by adding additional theme areas and self-contained sports complexes and hotels, Walt Disney World has attempted to monopolize not only the theme park consumer but the entire entertainment dollar.

Yes. It's all true, good and bad. Minorities and women are given appallingly short shrift in even the latest re-edited versions of the *American Adventure* and *The Hall of Presidents* Audio-Animatronic shows. On the other hand, Disney has also provided insurance benefits to same-sex partners (an act for which it has taken hits from conservative groups); closes the gates for the annual Gay and Lesbian Day in June, which attracts an estimated 60,000 guests; and refashioned its old Universe of Energy program as a vehicle for gay comic Ellen DeGeneres, whose show formerly ran on the Disney-owned ABC. The company has been both intent and imaginative when it comes to expanding its fiscal base, taking on corporate co-sponsors, beating competitors to the promotional punch, and especially catering to the increased spending power of the over-35 generation.

It's also fair to emphasize the blinkering effects of such total-package marketing. But something more ornate than mere symbolism is operating here. Walt Disney World reawakens the child in us by providing that extraordinary and undifferentiated stimulation—fantastic, scientific, emotional, projected, fearsome, heroic—that for most people is available only in their youth. Educational programs and museum-quality exhibits abound; the detailed furnishings and decor of the various parks are incredibly accomplished and fascinating, if only in a weird, kitsch-culture way; the menu of thrill rides and amusements offered says reams about American pop culture, if you are inclined to muse while standing in line; and the park's undeniable magnetism for tourists of all ages is itself a sociological marvel. At least a dozen languages can be heard not only at Epcot but all over the World.

The park is increasingly interactive, as the Imagineers would say. The areas where the experience is the most passive in Fjellman's sense are the older ones, the ones connected to the fairy tales and the American-nostalgia settings that were the original basis of the vision: the Magic Kingdom, Cinderella Castle, Frontierland, etc. But much of the later areas, designed not merely for parents but for adults as individuals, are far more sophisticated, especially in their psychological aspects, than those in the older, simpler, more specifically child-amusement days.

"Rides" is an almost laughably inadequate term for these full-sensory simulations. You *are* there, in sometimes terrifying ways. When one takes the Body Wars ride in the Wonders of Life Pavilion at Epcot (which uses entirely convincing physical effects as well as visual cues to induce the sensations of motion, speed, and even vertigo), the vast pulsing we are subjected to, momentarily "trapped" in the valve of an artery, taps our deepest ambiguities about the mysteries of the heart itself. We are not only coming as close to real medical wonders as most of us will ever get, but we are momentarily exposed to what a lot of Zen scholars and contemplatives have been after all their lives: rebirth. We are hearing that heartbeat, vibrating to it, in the overwhelming way we did in the womb. It is scary, it is astonishing—and it should be, for any intelligent adult, a prescient reminder of our real humanity.

The theatrically produced rides at Walt Disney World more usefully answer the emotional needs of children, those in grade school particularly, than mindless roller coasters or "monster rides." The scary parts—the ghosts and bones and occasional apparent death or animal struggle—are dealt with in an imaginative and often humorous way. (Walt Disney himself, whose true-nature animal films were among his most successful, never shrank from showing real-life violence—although he wasn't so open-minded about sex.)

Yet even when these scary characters are not comic, they're arousing. The transformation of Maleficent, the evil fairy in *Sleeping Beauty,* into a dragon is one of the most chilling and artistically perfect sequences in animation history (and sums up more neatly than any Bettelheim essay the metaphorical power of nightmare); the moral, that her destruction by the Prince is a victory of right over might and good over evil, is made more satisfying by its tension.

But it *is* a victory. At the end of the Disney frights there is always safety, reward, heroism, redemption. Compare that to the body counts of Freddy Krueger's and Jason's endless massacres. Remember, too, that a lot of the characters created or re-created at Disney World are allowed to be imperfect: Indiana Jones can be vain and pigheaded; apprentice sorcerer Mickey is lazy and disobedient (and gets bailed out by the stern paternal magician); and so on.

It is certainly true that Walt Disney World lays a veneer of cultural referencing over every aspect of the park, not only in the amusements but in hotels and dining rooms. But these references have grown steadily broader and more, well, multicultural.

It may be the most infuriating ride in history, at least in terms of its theme song, but It's a Small World, created for the 1964 World's Fair, was at least a well-intentioned salute to what we now call the global village. The pavilions of Epcot's World Show-case are the equal of any World's Fair offering, and in at least a few cases arts and traditions that are vanishing in the real world—the delicate and reticent juggler outside the Japan pavil-ion suggests one—are being conserved in the Disney world.

If it's true that Disney World is sometimes reactive or frankly greedy in its planning and design—imitating major film hits, adding New Orleans– or Key West– or New England–style attractions as those destinations become trendy—it is certainly not alone. In fact, some of those cities are re-creating themselves to attract the same sort of tourist business. If the Disney World resorts are artificial, if a turn-of-the-century wilderness lodge, Cape Cod cottage, Santa Fe adobe, and a luau cove aren't indige-nous to central Florida, what does that matter? People shell out huge sums of money not just to stay at Robert Redford's Sun-dance resort but to buy furniture from its catalogue and decorate their homes with mechanically weathered cupboards and wrought-iron gates. And in truth, these fantasy getaways can be more restorative and probably more informative than vacations to real but, to inexperienced travelers, loud, crowded, smoky, and unintelligible foreign countries.

Even more important, the Disney "universe," far from offering only escape from the so-called real world, offers techniques for solving many of our everyday frustrations. Yes, Walt Disney wanted total control of his Florida kingdom because he was infu-riated by the gaudy development that crowded up around his first park in Anaheim. Yes, the company has used its muscle shame-lessly to get advantageous zoning decisions, highway improve-ments, and tax credits—and not always either tactfully or perhaps straightforwardly. (In the inadvertently telling phrase of Stephen Joseph Rabori, who offered his master's thesis in planning at the University of Tennessee on the park's design in 1993, "Walt Dis-ney World has tested the authority of government" in its drive to reinvent infrastructure and management.)

But Walt Disney's broader concerns about what he saw taking place in Eisenhower-boom California—the increasing pollution, the decrepit housing, the widening social division, the auto-centric transportation planning—led him to develop methods of public transportation, ecologically beneficent plantings, and conflict-free crowd control. His mandate to protect the environment—observed to an extent almost unheard of in its day—led to the park's sophisticated water control and energy-efficiency techniques, and to the establishment of more than 7,500 acres of permanent wilderness preserve and the 11-acre Discovery Island wildlife sanctuary in Bay Lake. In 1992, Disney purchased the 8,500-acre Walker Ranch and turned it over to the Nature Conservancy, a deal that admittedly benefited the company but helped the restoration effort just as much.

If Walt Disney World reminds us of the responsibilities of violence-free society, all the better. What else is going to drive us to protest violence or help us teach our children consideration? The civility that is so often remarked on—the willingness of people to wait in line, to make allowances for young children, to smile, and to speak politely—may begin as a sort of park "peer pressure," but civility, like anything else, is a matter of reinforcement. Once practiced—once enjoyed—it is more apt to become habitual.

If so many of Disney's film and television characters are used to raise the park's profile among young children and to reinforce the urge to buy Disney-specific souvenirs, that's a commodity trap worth remembering (or at least budgeting for). But what are the alternatives? Every children's show, even *Sesame Street* and *The Muppets,* has marketing tie-ins, and most are far less innocent than T-shirts and stuffed animals. Considering the amount of violence in such shows as *X-Men* and *Pokémon,* the Teenage Mutant Ninja Turtles—acrobatic tao-boys with Renaissance painters' names and pizza joneses—are a relatively benign addition to Mr. Disney's Neighborhood.

Even in the "hidden" world that Fjellman wants us to keep in mind as evidence of manipulation, there are more universal parallels. When I think of the network of utility tunnels under the castle, I remember the catacombs of Rome and the sewers of Paris; I think of the efforts of architects and urban planners to increase the "livability" of real cities by using just the same sort of concealed power lines and service corridors; I think of the body itself, with all its myriad wonders of blood vessels and tendons and muscles; and I view the park as the imagination set free to walk.

All of this is not to say "Pay no attention to the man behind the curtain." Indeed, this book is primarily about the Wizard, and how he chose to offer us that heart (Fantasyland), or that brain (Epcot), or that nerve (Body Wars). Of course he has a darker side, a corporate agenda. But his real gift has been to keep alive our sense of adventure and, at his best, our sense of wonder. As Dorothy and her friends learned by taking the Yellow Brick Road—an odyssey re-created in The Great Movie Ride at Disney-MGM Studios—the destination is more often within you than without. We're all going to Walt Disney World, it seems, so keep a smile on your face and your hands inside the boat.

In the Beginning

The Buying of Walt Disney World

It was almost kismet—Kismet, Florida. But even then, it might not have been big enough for Walt Disney's dream.

Walt Disney World is more than 30,000 acres, or 48 square miles. That's more than 80 times the size of Monaco. Grace Kelly would have been queen of a larger and wealthier kingdom if she'd married Uncle Walt instead of Prince Rainier.

But the vastness of Walt Disney World was no happy accident. Disney had made one mistake building his first kingdom—not building a big enough "moat" around it—and he wasn't about to make it with the second one. "One thing I learned from Disneyland," Walt Disney once groused, "was to control the environment." Almost as soon as Disneyland opened in 1955, motel operators, fast-food franchises, and tacky souvenir shops tried to camp as close to the castle door as possible. The entrance to the Anaheim park is on Harbour Boulevard, and that jerry-built, neon-splattered strip became the company's version of the Alamo: "Never again!"

After watching what happened to the periphery of Disneyland once the get-rich-quick jackals moved in, Walt Disney was determined that the next time he would control the visual horizon in every direction, no matter how much land it took. The illusion, the controlled perspective, would not blur even at the edges. That has remained one of the most remarkable aspects of the park today. Despite its (now) urbanized location, Walt Disney World seems to exist entirely apart from any city, as if the Orlando airport, with its monorail-like transit system and its immaculate cleanliness, were the first terminal of this new World. Once inside the "perimeter"—and even that sounds like some futuristic containment center—no concrete skyscrapers, no truck exhaust, no billboards, no power lines interrupt the perfect sky (except those at the Marketplace, and they run through a suspiciously familiar-shaped "pole").

In fact, with what most of those Anaheim entrepreneurs would have considered an insane waste of buildable space, Disney World has kept huge stretches of the park near the highways as green buffer zones, allowing the eye and the mind to forget the scale and even the shape of the outside world. The first construction you actually reach after leaving Interstate 4 are hotels, but from the fantastic furbelows, columns, and Claus Oldenberg–sized golf tees—and the giant swans, dolphins, and Triton's horns lavished on them—you'd take them for fairy tale sets at the least.

An unblemished vista wasn't the only consideration, of course: Disney wanted to hold enough territory to exercise total control over development in the practical sense as well. For one thing, in the first decade that Disneyland was open, the merchants in the area just outside the park bled off an incredible amount of the entertainment dollars that would otherwise have been spent inside. By one estimate, the exploiters made twice the money Disney did. Dealing with Anaheim's local utilities cost him a fortune as well: he had to pay for installing power lines a second time in order to have them buried underground.

So, for Disney, the aesthetics and the economics went hand in hand. That meant finding a large enough tract of undeveloped, or at least minimally developed, land that at the same time would be accessible—under Disney's own terms—to the millions of people he needed to attract. The site needed to be in a fairly warm climate so that it could operate year-round. That eliminated such early suggestions as Niagara Falls, Baltimore, and Washington, DC (although in the mid-1990s, the Disney Company embarked on another preliminary land-buying binge for an American history park outside D.C. before other wealthy landowners with better-connected lobbyists blocked it).

Disneyland's success was so great that any number of cities tried to interest Walt in a joint venture. Among the more serious contenders was a group of developers in St. Louis who were looking for a tourist draw along the Mississippi riverfront; Disney considered their proposal fairly seriously until beer magnate Adolph Busch stood up at a business dinner and demanded the park sell beer. Not only did that scotch the St. Louis location, Walt Disney prohibited the sale of any alcohol anywhere in Walt Disney World—a prohibition that lasted until the mid-1980s. (Although alcohol is increasingly obvious around other areas of the park, as discussed in "Pleasure World," it is still prohibited in the Magic Kingdom.)

Orlando wasn't even the only part of the state Disney considered. He had traffic surveys and forecasts prepared for the entire region, which began to pinpoint the central "girdle" where the Florida Turnpike links I-4, I-75 (then in the planning stages), and I-10. Although the state had endured a series of building booms and land sale frauds so notorious that the Marx Brothers set their comedy *Cocoanuts* around it, the middle stretches were still largely undeveloped and could be had relatively cheap. Disney prospectors seriously evaluated a large tract along the border of Martin and Palm Beach as well as the Osceola-Orange area.

In fact, Walt even considered coming home—to Kismet, Florida, a then tiny and now vanished town in Volusia County where his parents were married. Although Walt himself was not born there (his parents had moved to Chicago after the collapse of the citrus industry, just before the turn of the century), he had family there and had visited several times as a child. (Volusia is also where Ponce de León landed in his search for the Fountain of Youth; maybe he should have tried Orlando.)

But it was the beauty of the area itself—the mixture of pasture, forest, and marsh—that finally sold Walt Disney on his future kingdom. In 1964, when Disney had his pilots swing the corporate Gulfstream over the pine swamps of central Florida, he pointed out a spot about 15 miles south of Orlando where an unfinished expressway (soon to be the Florida Turnpike) was scraping toward I-4. Then Disney caught a glimpse of a little island in the blue of Bay Lake. "Great," he pronounced. "Buy it." (That island is now the abandoned Discovery Island; perhaps someday it will return to the state it was in when Walt first admired it.)

Disney also quickly dispensed with the Harbour Boulevard problem. When at one early meeting his brother Roy, the financial fall guy, objected to buying yet more land, saying, "We already own about 12,500 acres," Walt shot back: "Two questions: Is the price right? Do we have the money?"

"Yes to both," his brother conceded.

"Okay," Walt said, ending the discussion. "How would you like to own 10,000 acres next to Disneyland right now?"

But even that didn't quite satisfy Walt. "If he could have," one of his key staffers said later, "he would have bought 50,000 acres."

Florida B.D.: Before Disney World

Before it was Walt Disney World, central Florida was primarily agricultural, a combination of cattle ranches, orange groves, and cypress swamps filled with alligators, wild hogs, deer, bobcats, heavenly colored birds, and hellishly avid bugs. It was also notoriously prone to economic boom-and-bust cycles, a history that perhaps added in the 1960s to some local skeptics' dread of the Disney invasion.

The Orlando area shook off a little swamp dust in the 1880s, when the first railroad was laid and farmers discovered the commercial potential of the native citrus groves. It bit that dust for the first time only a few years later, when back-to-back freezes at the end of 1894 and the early weeks of 1895 wiped out the crop and killed off most of the trees. (About the same time, Hamilton Disston bought four million acres of the Everglades for two bits an acre and set about draining them.) Many of the farmers and homesteaders left the area, including Walt Disney's parents.

A second boom, this one based on the real estate business and even more feverishly inflationary, puffed up Florida after World War I. The combination of affordable automobiles, cheap land, and hospitable climate pushed land prices into the skies. Ponzi-style speculators made small down payments on huge lots and then sold off the land, at even more extravagant prices, to outlanders who mooned over idealized and often completely fictional land brochures. Orlando authorities issued building permits worth more than $8.5 million in 1925; there were nearly 5,000 realtors, at least so-called, in that city alone. Miami/Dade County's land fever was running even higher.

But the first shock wave that ran through the New York stock market in 1926 cracked that fragile facade. The National Better

Business Bureau began investigating the fraudulent real estate promotions, and a devastating hurricane that killed nearly 400 people and laid waste to most of Miami and southern Florida knocked the "paradise" vision on its end. Bankruptcies and foreclosures became routine; the city slashed its budget; and the Chamber of Commerce nearly went under.

Things remained fairly quiet until after World War II, when a more genteel, monied group of summer resort hotels opened, catering to the likes of the Astors and Rockefellers. The Orlando's area's lake and beaches were studded with rent-a-canoe docks and public ballrooms, but it still trailed well behind Miami and the Keys as a vacation spot.

Space technology companies that were moving into the Canaveral neighborhood had fueled a smallish but comfortable regional boom in the late 1950s, beginning with Martin-Marietta and its Pershing missiles plant. But they were already beginning to lay off workers. And it was clear from the shrinking crowds that the space program was already losing its novelty. Even the resort havens of Sarasota, Tampa, and Daytona Beach flourished only seasonally. There was already a semi-official retirement industry, but in those days senior citizens were not considered or courted as consumers. (That particular inspiration of Disney's—to invent a theme park that would not only accommodate older patrons but actively attract them and exploit their relative wealth of leisure time—has since become one of his most emulated innovations.) And after all, in the 1960s most trend-trackers were focusing on the New American Youth, not their grandparents.

By 1964, the Orlando area had as its only major tourist draw the former Cape Canaveral, then only recently and mournfully rechristened the Kennedy Space Center in honor of the president whose assassination seemed to symbolize the sudden choking off of the nation's postwar vitality and assurance. By the time Disney began feeling out the Florida market, Orlando was ripe for yet another round of development.

The "Mystery Buyer"

From the moment they settled on the Orlando area as their preferred site, it was obvious to Disney and his "Compass East" project team that the company's name must be kept quiet as long as possible to prevent land prices inflating out of reach. So real estate and mortgage agents were hired through layers of dummy developers; many smaller transactions were handled in cash; and correspondence was routed through a post office box address in Kansas City. High-ranking executives traveled under pseudonyms; Disney himself favored the name "Bill Davis." Lawyers representing such dummy firms as Florida Ranch Lands, Latin American Development and Management Corp., and the original Reedy Creek Ranch Corp. began combing through land records, looking for large parcels and potentially willing sellers.

The first crucial contact that Disney representatives made, however, was with Billy Dial, then president of the First National Bank at Orlando. It was to be the making of both Disney World, which financed its construction through Dial and his alliance, and of the institution, now SunTrust, one of the dominant banks in the region and the only one that operates— with its tellers in turn-of-the-century Main Street costume— within Disney World itself.

The second crucial interview was, at Dial's urging and to Disney's surprise, with then publisher Martin Andersen of the *Orlando Sentinel.* (Dial had previously been an attorney for the *Sentinel* and remained a close friend and confidant of Andersen.) Disney attorneys told Andersen that rumors of the move had already surfaced in California, and they were concerned it might spread to Florida before they were ready to announce. Amazingly, Andersen agreed to delay publicizing or publicly speculating on the mysterious purchasers until most of the essential lots were in hand. In fact, he even agreed not to disclose the Disney connection to his own reporting staff, and ordered his key editorial staffers to do the same.

In many cases, the land booms of earlier decades paid belated dividends to the Disney team. Much of the lakefront land had been sold by mail order catalogue in 1913, and Disney's dummy companies were often able to take advantage of the casual ignorance of landowners who had never seen their holdings, had inherited them or had had them transferred through business swaps, or who had found themselves in possession of a swamp or forest they could never afford to develop. Disney's plan was to buy up smaller parcels from absentee owners and take options on crucial major tracts.

The first really large purchase was from the legendary Florida state senator Irlo "Bud" Bronson in late 1964; he sold 8,380 acres of base scrub and swamp for a little over $100 an acre—and on a handshake deal at that. (Later, when the identity of the purchaser was made public, Bronson's son asked him about backing out, but the senator said he had to stick by his word.) Not until May 1965, when that deed of sale and one other were recorded by the Osceola County Clerk, did the first *Sentinel* story appear—with a pointed warning against "speculation" as to the identity of the mystery client.

Most of the early rumors, in fact, centered on the space industry and aviation companies: Lockheed, Howard Hughes, McDonnell Douglas, Republic, PhilCo. At least one television announcer fell victim to jokesters who sent him an urgent telegram that said the mystery buyer was Ford Motor Company. He interrupted the telecast to read it on camera. There were great congratulations on-screen, but a few minutes later the follow-up telegram arrived: "They want to pasture out their Mustangs."

More suspects were tossed about: Great Lakes Steel, Boeing, General Electric, Chrysler, Volkswagen, even the Rockefeller family. The *Sentinel* itself, in an astonishing bit of prevarication that it spent years having to live down, published a story that did refer to the notion that "the land is being purchased for a second East Coast Disneyland attraction." But they announced that "little credence is being given this in view of the fact that Walt Disney himself, in a recent statement to the *Orlando Sentinel* while on a visit to Cape Kennedy, said he was spending $50 million to expand his California attraction and . . . had his hands full."

Only three days later, however, the paper admitted in an editorial that it had not only promised not to reveal the company's identity, but had helped the company buy a 35-acre tract "they wanted and needed." By the end of May, the rival *Evening Star* had uncovered a $5 million package of 47 purchases made through an Orlando brokerage firm, totaling 27,250 acres. In effect, Disney had purchased his kingdom for less than $200 an acre; within months, would-be carpetbaggers were paying around $40,000 an acre, with prime tracks going for five or six times that.

Andersen managed to keep the Disney name a close secret for five months, until one of his more dogged reporters, Emily Bavar, editor of the *Sentinel's* Sunday magazine, caught Walt Disney himself off guard during an interview in California. By then, rather than categorically deny the question, Disney merely replied, "I'd rather not say," which, as any reporter knows, is an affirmative response. Bavar immediately wrote that the mystery investor was Disney.

Bavar's story was intentionally underplayed by the *Sentinel's* management, but even so, it was clear the time had come to let the mouse out of the bag. On October 24, 1965, the *Sentinel* ran another editorial, this one exuberantly pro-Disney and pro-development. The adjectives used included "fantastic," "fabulous," and "prosperous." It promised that Orlando would become "the greatest tourist city in the world" and that the benefits would be universal. "The magic of this modern Merlin will touch us all here in this promised land of prosperity." That the details of this "fabulous" plan were still entirely secret didn't seem to bother anyone at the time. The next day, then Governor Haydon Burns, who had also been in on the secret from the beginning, made the formal announcement at the convention of the Florida municipal league in Miami.

A Mouse in the House (of Representatives)

Over the next year, the future World was largely a matter of political feint and parry. Disney, still committed to the rule of total control, blanketed the state legislature with lobbyists and consultants polishing friendly statutes, particularly on the subject of highway improvements. In the beginning, Florida voters turned down a road bond issue worth $300 million that would have paid for many of those improvements. Although it was not a particularly anti-Disney vote, just an anti-tax one, it apparently surprised the self-absorbed Disney corporation—and sounded the first warning to state residents that they wouldn't be getting this tourist industry treasure trove without investing a few coins themselves.

But on December 15, 1966, Walt Disney, who had been battling lung cancer, died of complications. Despite the corporation's assurances, Disney's death threatened to break the political spell. So in February 1967, the Disney organization gathered its forces in nearby Winter Haven for a final strategic push. Before an audience including Florida governor Claude Kirk and his cabinet, the state legislature, business leaders, and media, the corporation laid out a plan including a Disneyland-like amusement park, theme motels, sports and recreational areas "which will take advantage of and preserve the natural beauty of the area," an industrial park for state-of-the-art technologies, and a jetport to handle private charters and "executive planes."

It also, for the first time, mentioned the "Experimental Prototype Community of Tomorrow, planned for 20,000 permanent residents." That prototype, Epcot, was the main subject of a prerecorded 25-minute video starring Walt Disney himself—a sort of sales pitch from beyond the grave. While most of us are more familiar with Walt from the vault than the man himself, thanks to those TV clips and even the bits of video still used at the parks, on that day, less than two months after his death, his obvious sincerity and conviction made a strong impression on his official audience.

Disney called Epcot "the heart of everything we'll be doing."

Epcot, he went on, "will never be completed, but will always be introducing and testing and demonstrating new materials and systems . . . We're convinced [that] the need is not just for curing old ills of old cities, or even just building a whole new shiny city. We think the need is for starting from scratch on virgin land like this, and building a special kind of community . . . Everything in Epcot will be dedicated to the happiness of the people who live here and work here [as well as] those who come here from all around the world."

That influx of tourists, historians have pointed out, was the bait. Then came the hook: "We must have the flexibility . . . to work in cooperation with American industry, and to make decisions based on standards of performance. If we have this kind of freedom, I'm confident we can create a world showcase for American free enterprise that will bring new industry to the state of Florida from all over the country." In other words, don't tangle us up with red tape and we'll make enough money for both of us.

Governor Kirk agreed, saying the state would garner $4 billion in tourist income in the first ten years alone, plus additional revenues from new construction and permanent service jobs. (He was too conservative: in 1981, an *Orlando Sentinel* business reporter said that Disney World had "stimulated economic activity in its first year to a degree originally forecast more than ten years in the future.") Kirk was among early boosters who helped Disney put a pretty face on its iron control by supporting its proposal to combine its holdings into the Reedy Creek Improvement District—to become its own government. On May 12, 1967, Governor Kirk signed the bills establishing the Reedy Creek entity; he called "the magic moment that Walt and Roy Disney decided to make Florida their second home a landmark in Florida history equaled only by the arrival of Ponce de León and the opening of the railroad to Palm Beach." That same day, the state road board voted to divert $5 million over the next five years to start on highway improvements near the park.

At the local level, however, politicians felt a little less enthusiastic about the sort of legislative flexibility the company was talking about. In effect, Disney was going over the heads of both Osceola County and Orange County to zone, develop, tax, and administer itself. One big savings to Disney, for example, was in impact fees that one local commissioner estimated would have cost more than $18 million per hotel (in 1971 dollars, at that).

By 1967, *Orlando Sentinel* publisher Andersen had either had time to think things through in more depth or at least to be embarrassed into rediscovering his journalistic objectivity. The *Sentinel* began to run stories and editorials questioning whether the state was really ready to absorb such a huge and revolutionary project, and speculating on the potential drawbacks of granting Reedy Creek such autonomy.

They had a point. In the early years especially, Walt Disney World had a pretty high-handed attitude toward the state and local governments. Instead of expanding a twisting, old, two-lane delivery road that was supposedly the employee entrance, Disney launched a public relations campaign calling the road dangerous and finally forcing the state to have it rebuilt. One Orange County commission estimated that by the time the park opened in 1971, Walt Disney World had cost the county

$12–14 million in funds that had to be withdrawn from previously okayed improvements. A later flap over state bonds that Reedy Creek obtained for development was even more bitter: the bonds had certainly been legally obtained, but many felt Disney was not living up to the spirit of the agreement, especially since several other jurisdictions had planned to use the bonds for low-cost housing and other social welfare programs.

Disney's presence did make land many times more valuable than it had been, but that also meant painful increases in tax assessments for residents. Many longtime ranchers had to sell off their lands because of the inflated taxes. Disney, itself the beneficiary of so many special exceptions, fought a very long battle against the Orange County assessor to get its taxes lowered, giving it a reputation for corporate egocentricity that it has never quite shaken.

Nevertheless, Disney has unquestionably been an economic boon to Orlando, turning the entire region into a prime investment market and one of the top tourist destinations anywhere. Its property taxes add scores of millions to local budgets every year. Every time a new resort or theme park is built and opens, thousands of new construction and permanent jobs are added to the regional economy; even in times of general recession, the unemployment rate around Orlando has been extraordinarily low.

And over the last several years the Disney Company has worked hard to improve its community image, handing out grants (with plenty of publicity) and establishing minority programs, albeit under some pressure. To soothe concerns over previous animal rights debacles (see "Animal, Vegetable, or Mineral?"), Disney has set up an advisory board of wildlife and conservation experts to oversee its plans for a wild animal park. Its Celebration community (see "The Mouse That Scored: The Michael Eisner Era") produces an estimated $42 million a year in property taxes, more than doubling Osceola County's revenues.

"They're actually much better now," as one businessman put it. "They used to say, 'Hey, we made you what you are.' Now it's, 'Remember, we have to live here, too.'"

The manager of a nearby hotel franchise, interviewed by the *Sentinel,* took Disney's building of budget hotels in stride. "This is a capitalistic society. I look at it this way: if Disney wasn't here, we'd all be sitting in orange groves."

The Vision Comes into Focus

When Walt Disney first contemplated his eastern kingdom, he recognized that even if he succeeded in getting the state to take a hands-off approach to the project, it would be best to get the construction physically under way as quickly and smoothly as possible—demonstrating that his company was as cutting-edge as promised while effectively squelching any protests before they had time to arise.

To do that, he hired a pair of engineering experts with experience in the snap-to world of the armed services: former Army Corps of Engineers major general William E. "Joe" Potter, who had been Robert Moses' second-in-command at the New York World's Fair, and retired Admiral Joe Fowler, who had also headed up the construction at Disneyland. Fowler's presence tipped off at least one Orlando real estate broker, who was driving one of the dummy-company attorneys around town. The broker heard his passenger address a companion as "Admiral," and that night he spotted a photograph in a *National Geographic* story profiling Fowler as "the man who built Disneyland." Fortunately for Disney, the broker kept his sleuthing to himself.

As Walt Disney began to expand his vision of the site to include not only the park itself but a sort of science-and-tech Utopia, he gave himself a crash course in planning, technology, and what would now be considered market research. He had Potter send letters to 500 foundations and research centers and set up 100 personal visits. He toured shopping malls and pedestrian centers and read the latest reports on urban planning and environmental advances. Battling cancer, he researched cryonics, the freezing of human bodies for future defrosting and, presumably, healing. This fascination led to one of Walt Disney World's most resilient myths: that Disney himself is lying in icy state in an upper room of Cinderella Castle.

By the time Walt died, he had pretty much set the tone for the park's wide-ranging interests: the solar and even nuclear-power experiments, sustainable agriculture, and robotic and synthetic "life."

In 1968, the Disney Company raised $90 million in bond sales for construction and took out a line of credit worth $50 million from a consortium of banks (although, since the company stock kept going up, virtually all its debts were paid before the park was complete).

The company forged an agreement with the labor unions in 1969 that ensured a strike-free project in return for swift good-faith negotiation of disagreements. There was another trade-off involved: Disney proposed to pay lower wages than some other Florida developers, but it did promise to hire through the unions. That, in the long run, was more important to the AFL-CIO.

Opening day was set for October 1, 1971. But in 1970 the California-based construction firm said the park would not, could not, be ready on time. But the farm, so to speak, had all been mortgaged; the show had to go on. So the construction firm was fired, and a little financial sleight of hand allowed Disney to lease the equipment and take on the job itself. It came close to failing: Dick Nunis, then director of operations and later president of the park, told the *Sentinel* that in the last weeks he suddenly realized no worker was expecting to come in on Labor Day. Gritting his teeth, Nunis was inspired to invite the workers and their families to picnic at the unfinished park, and they worked with renewed dedication for the rest of the time.

About two months before the opening, *Life* magazine sent out a photographer to take a picture. Despite the looming deadlines, Disney executives decided to take the fullest advantage of the publicity. They called up the entire cast of characters in full costume and makeup, from the Mouse to the Seven Dwarfs, and posed them in front of Cinderella Castle. All the musicians, greeters, ride attendants, cooks, and even the street sweepers were lined up behind them. The *Life* photographer, in the style of those days, set up spots and extra lighting to excise any potential shadows (it was full sunlight and pushing 100°, according to some reports), and then, hoisted overhead in a cherry picker, he began to take test shots and light measurements. Hours passed. Various cast members fainted and had to be replaced by newly costumed and made-up characters, and Nunis fumed and paced. Finally, photographer Yale Joel took one perfect frame—and it is still one of the best covers that ever graced that photophile magazine. It ran on October 15, 1971.

Ten days or so before the opening, a group of national tourist executives and legislators came for a tour; they were "flabbergasted," one remembers, but they did wonder where all the trees were. Requests for interviews, free tickets, and charity appearances came so fast and furious that one secretary finally screamed, "I can't take it anymore!" and tossed her telephone right through the wall.

One *Sentinel* reporter sneaked into *The Hall of Presidents* on the last day, claiming to be part of the work crew. When he finished his shift, he walked out toward what had been a flat field—it had turned into a grassy hill. The night before, or rather the morning of, the grand opening, the head of publicity finally went home at 1 a.m., the press room had no telephones and no typewriters, no floor coverings, no wallpaper, and only a few light bulbs. But when he returned at 5 a.m., the press center was ready.

On opening day everyone involved in the project was frantic. At 10 a.m. another intrepid reporter discovered that the paint on the walls of the ice cream parlor was still wet. National predictions that the park would draw huge crowds—or fail if it didn't—had Disney employees dizzy and dreading disaster.

The park neither drew a huge crowd nor failed. On that first morning, despite a swarm of traffic helicopters and state troopers, only about 9,000 paying guests showed up, met by 5,000 frantically smiling employees. Some Disney veterans claim that the "soft opening" was intentional, that they had picked a slow month and a slow day, Friday, so that the cast would have time to work out the kinks. But most kept their fingers crossed for the holidays, and sure enough, on the Friday after Thanksgiving more than 200,000 would-be guests were stalled in traffic on I-4. The park had to close the gate by mid-morning. And on December 29, less than three months after its opening, the Magic Kingdom was packed with 69,500 visitors.

It was the beginning of the World.

Walt's World A.D.: After Disney

In the tense months of 1967 right after Walt Disney's death, when the kingdom was suddenly without its chief visionary, the company's key executives agonized over whether it would be possible to build the park without him. Roy Disney, who had been planning to retire, finally said, "Can we do it without Walt? We don't know—but let's try. And remember, we're not going to spend one penny over $125 million." The Magic Kingdom would wind up costing more than three times that.

But what the park earned blew away most predictions, too. In its first year, according to corporate reports, the park made a profit of nearly $22 million, which was just about what the financially acute Roy Disney had predicted. The next year profits rose to $40 million; and by 1980, they had doubled again. In its first ten years Walt Disney World made nearly $2.5 billion. By 1987 it had one-year profits of $450 million, and it makes more than twice that now.

Figures of attendance to Walt Disney World also went way beyond the Disney brothers' expectations. Forty million people visited Walt Disney World in its first four years, and a total of 125 million visited in its first ten years. But that was just the beginning: in 1995, Walt Disney World welcomed its 500 millionth guest.

In the early 1990s, when the Persian Gulf War pushed gasoline prices up and new entertainment meccas beckoned in Branson, Missouri, and Myrtle Beach, Disney World attendance stalled and even declined a bit. By 1994 attendance was down 5%—a drop most Orlando-area executives and analysts blamed on new chairman Michael Eisner's decision to hike ticket prices. However, toward the end of that year Eisner announced a new marketing strategy with a $116-million budget, and Disney opened its first budget hotels, the All-Star Sports and All-Star Music resorts. By 1995 attendance at Walt Disney World was back up an estimated 15% to 34 million visitors. Attendance figures generally continued to increase—in 1998, the Magic Kingdom alone pulled in 15.6 billion people—and that was not even a record.

Things haven't looked quite as rosy in recent months. Attendance at all theme parks, not just Disney's, slumped dramatically from 2000 to 2001, down 4% at the Magic Kingdom and down 15% at Epcot—perhaps reflecting the number of foreign visitors who usually head for the World Showcase. The post-9/11 slump was even more dramatic, of course (as much as a 20% drop in attendance through the end of the year), leading to construction slowdowns and cast layoffs. However, the parks are still among the high spots in the Disney biz—it's the movie and TV divisions that have declined and forced the much-publicized (and unprece-dented) drop in stock value. See the chapters "The Mouse That Scored: The Michael Eisner Era" and "Pleasure World: The Adult Industry" for more on Disney outside the World.

The World According to Walt

Walt Disney's America

When Walt Disney talked about "children of all ages," he meant it literally. Walt Disney dreamed of building a place to take his own children that would bear no resemblance to the traditional beer gardens and midways, a place of innocent delight and inspiration. And what an adult holds dearest, what he hopes to convey to his children, is usually the things he himself cherished when young. The child is not only father to the man but to his children. So before entering Walt's ultimate "World," it's worth stopping to remember the world he grew up in: the world and especially the America that inspired him, and the one he tried to re-create in his parks.

The quarter-century before and the first decade after Walt Disney's birth spanned, fittingly, one of the greatest eras of "imagineering" in history. It was the heyday of the great expositions and the early World's Fairs: the Philadelphia Exhibition of 1876, the Columbian Exposition of 1893 in Chicago (on which Walt's father had a construction job), the Paris Expositions of 1889 and 1900. George Eastman's photographic paper replaced painfully slow glass plates, followed in increasingly short order by celluloid film, the box camera, and motion picture cameras. *(The Great Train Robbery,* generally considered the first real narrative movie, plays continuously in the Magic Kingdom—another part of the time warp that keeps Main Street permanently in a 1903 golden age.)* Freeze-frame photography revealed the wonders of the running man and stop-film cameras the potential of animation. H. G. Wells ruminated on time travel and Einstein on relativity.

The first electric submarines, and then the first diesel-powered ones, carried deep-sea explorers into that other great unknown.

It was, especially in America, the age of the legendary inventors: Alexander Graham Bell, the Wright brothers, Thomas Edison. Electrification wrought one of the greatest revolutions: the extension of daylight. The assembly line produced commodities, and they eventually produced the consumer. The first plastics were created, and the first synthetics. Steel mills were transforming what had been an agricultural-mercantile society into the beginnings of an industrial one—and at least in that one period, great fortunes did trickle down: Andrew Carnegie's money built a great public opera house and opened libraries all over the country.

It was the era of the transatlantic cruise, the Great Tour, and the travelogue. It was the era of personal freedom as well, of motorized bicycles, pneumatic tires, and internal combustion—and the names Diesel, Benz, Ford, and Rolls-Royce.

It was a time when we took for granted the great rivers and the Mississippi paddle wheelers and leaped over them to the captured frontier. It was the age of the Yukon gold rush, the land booms, and the homestead acts; the age of Chief Joseph, Geronimo, and the Indian reservations. It was the era of gunslingers and desperados whose exploits were exaggerated by penny-dreadful books of "frontier justice" and Judge Roy Bean. The buffalo herds were replaced by the cattle drives, and Buffalo Bill took his "Wild West Show" to Europe.

It was the beginning of the communications era: Alexander Graham Bell put the private citizen "on line" for the first time, followed by the telegraph system and radio transmission. It was the era of the shrinking globe, of the new steam engines and the great railroads that inexorably marked off America, Siberia, Canada, the "Orient," and the "Levant." It was the era of the explorer-hero, of Richard Burton, Livingston and Stanley, Amundsen and Peary. In the years before Disney's birth, Heinrich Schliemann uncovered Troy and Mycenae; when Disney was only 20, Howard Carter broke through, into the tomb of Tut. Gauguin went to Tahiti and the U.S. Army to Hawaii. It was the age of Suez and the Panama Canal, of *The Arabian Knights, Tarzan of the Apes,* and *King Solomon's Mines.*

It was the age of vast and even worldwide epidemics: typhoid (which struck Disney's father), tuberculosis (which brother Roy contracted), and the virulent influenza of 1918, which nearly killed Walt himself. But it was also the era of radioactivity and antiseptics, the control of yellow fever, and the application of X-rays.

It was a time that confused patriotism and nativism, the era of essential immigrant labor and reactionary anti-immigrant riots. It was a time of international violence, of assassinations and nationalist uprisings and anarchists. The Spanish-American War was engineered by newspaper tycoon and would-be kingmaker William Randolph Hearst. But it was also the era of Wilson's League of Nations, the first serious one-world view articulated in this country, and of the dedication of the Statue of Liberty.

It was the age of the first comic strips, and of the first newsreels. It was a golden age for children's literature: *Wind in the Willows* and *Peter Pan, The Jungle Book* and *Just-So Stories, Alice in Wonderland* and *Uncle Remus, Tom Sawyer* and *Treasure Island,* and *Kidnapped* and Howard Pyle's rousing versions of *Robin Hood* and *King Arthur*—stories Disney turned to when he began to make films. His first full-length feature was a version of "Snow White and the Seven Dwarves," a fairy tale he'd seen in a silent version in his early teens. Tchaikovsky's *Nutcracker* and *Sleeping Beauty* were instantly classics, and he remembered them, too.

All these images, all these national obsessions, romances, and heroes, and in particular all the explorers and inventors—everything except the plagues and the wars—reappear in the part of Walt's amusement park that was closest to his own vision: the Magic Kingdom. The symbols of various other countries in It's a Small World, which foreshadow many of the icons at the World Showcase, are straight out of those early newsreels: the Eiffel Tower, the Sphinx, the Acropolis, the Taj Mahal, Big Ben. Walt himself was a talented inventor (it was his multiplane camera, newly mounted for exhibit in "One Man's Dream" at Disney-MGM, that made convincing three-dimensional animation possible), and like his idols, he used several World's Fairs, starting with the 1939 New York fair, as stages to unveil his technological innovations. Like Carnegie, he sincerely believed that culture should be made available to the masses (a concept that resulted in the kitsch classic *Fantasia*). Like Eadweard Muybridge and

George Eastman, he pushed camera technology forward; like Benz and Bell, he dreamed of impulsive travel and instantaneous communication. These same images pop up again and again in the later attractions as well, although, as we'll see, the corporate offspring of Disney had slightly less romanticized views.

Walt's Own Early History

Walter Elias Disney was born almost with the 20th century, in 1901. He was the fourth and youngest son of a willing but unlucky man who repeatedly labored to save his own money, spent it on private ventures—a citrus grove in Florida, a cattle farm in Missouri (where Walt was born), a jelly factory in Chicago—and in between, when they failed, took on carpentry or small construction jobs. As a boy, Walt Disney knew the unforgiving face of the Midwest as well as its prodigious energies; Walt often recalled having struggled through terrifying predawn blizzards, delivering newspapers in Kansas City—the sort of schoolboy nightmare people usually tell whoppers about. He was not a quick student anyway, and the added strain of farm chores and getting up at 3 a.m. made him even less successful.

His father was a strict taskmaster who believed his sons' duty was to add to the family fortune, whether they worked at home or outside. When Walt was only six, his two oldest brothers retaliated by getting what they considered their fair share of the family bank account (and a little more) and leaving home. That left only Walt and Roy, and all the money from their newspaper routes and any summer jobs had to be turned over to their father—a detail *not* included in "One Man's Dream"; hagiography is a family matter, apparently. Walt had to sneak an extra bundle of papers to sell in order to buy even penny candy behind his father's back. By the time he was a teenager, the farm had gone broke again and the family had moved to Chicago. Walt, who only completed one year of high school, had discovered night classes at the Chicago Art Institute, where he drew the cartoons for the school paper, and he was in a hurry to escape.

Walt had spent one summer selling papers and peanuts on the Santa Fe Railroad, and though he was a spectacular commercial failure—he let himself be shortchanged and cheated with apparent frequency—he was crazy about the trains themselves, and more than a little vain of his shiny-buttoned uniform. In 1918, stretching his age a little, he enlisted in the ambulance corps and headed for Europe. But having arrived after the Armistice was signed, he went to France, where he made a scant living cartooning and painting GI posters and fake German souvenirs and decorations for the victorious American grunts.

When Walt returned, he tried to get a job with his old employer, the *Kansas City Star,* as a cartoonist. They wouldn't hire him as a truck driver. He and his friend Ub Iwerks finally did get jobs with an advertising agency, and in 1920 Walt persuaded a local cinema owner to buy his early animation efforts (short commentaries and timely items called "Laugh-O-Grams") to run as fillers. Like his father, Walt quickly sank all his money into an animation studio of his own; like his father, he quickly went broke. At age 21, bearing a half-finished animated feature called, interestingly, *Alice's Wonderland,* he and Iwerks struck out for California, hoping to find work in one of the commercial studios there. Shortly thereafter, he persuaded banker brother Roy to come in with them.

Walt didn't have to wait long for his commercial breakthrough, or so it seemed. Still in his mid-20s, he hit on the character of an earnest and perhaps slightly goofy rabbit with long floppy ears named Oswald, whose animated adventures were distributed along with films from Universal Pictures by a theater magnate named Charles Mintz. By 1928 there were Oswald candy bars and souvenirs, and Disney, who was a better idea man than draftsman, had hired a studio of animators to help him with the demand. But this first success as a professional animator also led to his first hard lesson in autonomy: When Disney went to ask for more money, he discovered that Universal had, in the fine print, obtained the rights to Oswald—and that, preparing for this moment, Mintz had hired away all but one of Disney's animators, Iwerks himself.

Walt didn't tell Roy that they were broke again immediately, but on the train home to California, the legend goes, he began doodling circles and sticks, and out of that came the Mouse (although, the early Mickey wasn't nearly so spherical as the later version; over time, as Topsy would say, he just "O"ed). One of the most famous bits of Mickey trivia is that Walt originally considered naming him Mortimer, but thankfully his wife

Lillian demurred—another detail not included in "One Man's Dream." Mortimer in fact showed up as an occasional rival to Mickey and sometime bad guy in later productions.

It was Lucky Lindbergh who literally got Mickey off the ground. Mickey's first film, laid out in 1929, portrayed him as a daredevil pilot in *Plane Crazy*, but *Steamboat Willie*—featuring Mickey at the helm of a great Mississippi paddle wheeler a la Mark Twain, and with Walt's own voice squeaking on the soundtrack—was released first, and so became Mickey's official debut. *Steamboat Willie* still runs at the Main Street moviehouse in the Magic Kingdom.

It surprises people now to discover that few of Disney's features were immediate commercial successes. *Snow White and the Seven Dwarfs* earned him a bank loan in 1939 by winning a special Academy Award, but it had cost him $6 million and three years' labor; even so, the next year, *Pinocchio's* poor reviews cut off his credit. *Fantasia*—Disney's 1940 attempt to wed pop (Mickey Mouse and *The Nutcracker Suite*) with high culture (*The Firebird* and Leopold Stokowski)—was a colossal flop the first time out, although it is a cult classic today. Starting with shorts in the late 1940s, the real-life nature films such as *The Living Desert* (1953) became almost as famous in Disney productions as the Mickey Mouse cartoons. But they were emergency money-makers at the time; the studio might well have gone under otherwise. It would certainly have gone under if *Cinderella* had not been such a massive hit in 1950. After Disneyland opened in 1955, however, there was little problem.

The one thing Walt never did after Oswald was to sell or surrender the rights to any film or market tie-in—not even to brother Roy, the company finance man, who stopped speaking to his brother for ten years over the issue of merchandising royalties. But it did mean keeping his own company safe from raiders. That early lesson in the value of total creative and marketing control became the guiding precept behind the making of Walt Disney World.

Walt's Moment in Time

Walt Disney had a dream, but he also had a lucky draw, historically speaking. What he wanted to create might not have been possible, at least not in the form he envisioned, at any other moment in American history.

The first concept parks in this country appeared about the middle of the 19th century, and the most famous, like Coney Island's Luna Park, flourished toward the turn of the century and into Walt's early years. They reflected major changes in American society, most importantly the appearance for the first time of a mass paying audience—a middle class with money and time to spare, and the social drive to indulge both—and the widespread installation of electricity. It was the fantastic possibilities of the lighted midway and the heightened thrills of electrically powered roller coasters that reinvigorated the amusement park. (Although the effects are "boosted" by more up-to-date techniques, it still comes down to flash and splash.)

In the late 1940s, when he began to contemplate creating a vacation park, Walt Disney had similar social currents to ride. The wartime and postwar economy had produced a national boom (especially for the new middle class). Americans were beginning to live longer, so there were more grandparents and extended families. The creation of the interstate highway system made attracting tourists from great distances feasible, even—in the early era of driving and family vacations—an exciting prospect. And the development of air conditioning made it as attractive to vacation inside a park setting as at the seaside or in the mountains.

On top of that, Disney himself had the most enticing product of all: escapism. His animated characters were already American institutions. New money, new methods, and what seemed to be unlimited resources: America was a market just waiting to be exploited.

But Walt himself didn't think of it as exploitation. He was a serious disciple of the American Dream, and he had in mind to act as its living proof. Mickey represented an honest product (this time, one Walt was going to hold on to), a pure spirit and a cheerful heart, and a sort of staggeringly simple pleasure in the exercise of the imagination. "When You Wish Upon a Star" might have been written as the Disney Bill of Rights: "Anything your heart desires will come to you." *That* was the America Walt Disney desired to re-create for his children. So when he designed the Magic Kingdom, Disney looked away from the present and its ambiguities and toward the idealized past and the even more ideal future.

There's a famous bit of dialogue in Lewis Carroll's *Alice through the Looking-Glass*:

> The rule is, "Jam tomorrow and jam yesterday—but never jam to-day."

> "It must come sometimes to 'jam to-day'," Alice objected.

> "No, it can't," said the Queen. "It's jam every other day: to-day isn't any other day, you know."

> "I don't understand you," said Alice. "It's dreadfully confusing!"

> "That's the effect of living backwards," the Queen said kindly: "it always makes one a little giddy first—"

> "Living backwards!" Alice repeated in great astonishment. "I never heard of such a thing!"

> "—but there's one great advantage in it, that one's memory works both ways."

Walt Disney looked into the future and back to the past, but he almost never seemed to find himself in the present. Most of the early attractions recalled, with an exaggerated nostalgia, the brighter eras and the heroes and romances of his childhood: the great explorers, the Wild West, the patriot fathers, the Industrial Revolution, the children's stories.

He especially loved the Victorian Era, calling it America's "innocent years." The Missouri of his childhood was theoretically the inspiration for Main Street, U.S.A., though only in its halcyon summer-vacation moments and stripped of any dismal memories: no blizzards, no doctor's office, and no schoolhouse. Almost no one has a dismal experience in Walt Disney's America, as a matter of fact— at least not that Walt noticed. (Disney World's white-male attitude toward history remains one of its weaker points, as discussed later in "America's Adventures in Wonderland.")

Almost every one of Walt Disney World's hotels and resort areas looks backward to some idealized past: Atlantic City between the wars, Florida during the first resort boom, wilderness America in its undeveloped sanctity, Gauguin's Polynesia, Crystal Palace Victoriana, Spanish Colonial California, Gilded Age Newport, the buccaneering Caribbean, even plantation-era Louisiana.

And it's just as well, because the odd thing is, like jam tomorrow, the "future" never actually arrives. The few futuristic attractions in Disney's original Tomorrowland were forward-looking only in the most romantic and simple fashion—that is, they were gussied-up versions of the past, just as *The Jetsons* was a recostumed imitation of *The Flintstones*. (In fact, check out the space-cadet uniforms on the line monitors at the *Alien Encounter*; they're straight out of *Flash Gordon*.) The moon rides and technological predictions were borrowed from 19th-century visionaries such as Jules Verne and H. G. Wells and even Edgar Allan Poe. Not surprisingly, many of Tomorrowland's attractions have lived not just full lives, but whole ones: "If You Had Wings," Star Jets, Flight to the Moon and its successor Mission to Mars have all come and gone (as has, for futuristic fans, "Captain EO").

Even the renovated Tomorrowland attractions are 99% past and 1% promise, from Spaceship Earth to the *Timekeeper* attraction. The *Timekeeper* even uses Verne and Wells as characters. The World of Motion exhibit in Future World at Epcot, which didn't get much farther into the future than moving sidewalks, has been replaced by Test Track, a thrill ride that doesn't even pretend to get out of the 1990s: It's a harrowing variation on seat-belt safety hosted by TV's most beloved fall guys, the crash-test dummies.

The Tomorrowland at Disneyland in California is also under renovation, for the third time in its 40 years. When the Imagineers went to Disney CEO Michael Eisner seeking guidance, he reportedly said to them, "How do you create the future when the future looks like Montana?" What he meant was that those very high-tech people movers and plastic furnishings that in Walt Disney's time spelled progress now seem harsh and impersonal. Eisner believes more and more Americans want to join the back-to-simplicity movement, heading away from the techno-heavy urban centers that were Tomorrowland's pretext—and his conviction is the reason that Disney's first residential development, Celebration, is being built not as a technological show-place but as a model small town, a true "community." (And also that Disneyland's first major expansion in years is "California Adventure." There's no place like home.)

At bottom, this future-past is a built-in paradox: Walt Disney World is full of rousing speeches about how much better technology is going to make our lives, and yet, by definition, the computers, vehicles, and imaging techniques we are seeing already exist. Certain transportation systems—unlimited space travel certainly—are still beyond us. But the concept is old—there is little new thinking on display. Perhaps this difficulty is one reason the Eisner-era Disney Company has moved away from futuristic predictions and into futuristic effects, like those at Disney-MGM Studios and *Alien Encounter,* or back to the equally mysterious but less rapidly evolving past, like the dinosaur world in the Animal Kingdom, or just to the day-to-day escapism of sports and self-fulfillment (see "Pleasure World"). And so the new Disneyland Tomorrowland focuses more on the *process* of creating the future than on any results.

The one truly progressive concept Walt Disney cherished was Epcot, his new city of tomorrow, and even that borrowed heavily—though he would have hated to hear it—from turn-of-the-century philosophy. In any case, Epcot, the gift Walt Disney envisioned as his legacy to future generations, was transformed by his corporate successors into just another huge pseudohistoric shopping mall, a permanent World's Fair or Exposition, before it ever broke ground. Maybe that's appropriate: Utopia yesterday, Utopia tomorrow, but never Utopia today.

The Mouse
That Scored

The Michael Eisner Era

It's tempting for those who grew up with the "old" Disney, the animated classics and the clean-cut Mouseketeers, to think of Michael Eisner as the "anti-Walt"—a guy with a corporate outlook instead of a creative one, a schemer rather than a dreamer. And it's true that Eisner has an enormously canny sense of the public appetite and how to feed it.

But, in fact, the two have more in common than traditionalists would like to admit. (After all, Walt Disney was no slouch when it came to forging an audience and spinning off side projects.) It was Disney who insisted on buying so much Florida land that it would take generations of development to use it all; Eisner was the one who launched the theme parks, resorts, professional sports franchises, and even residential communities that make the modern World. It was Disney who conceived of the all-ages attraction, and Eisner who understood how to exploit each segment of the expanding audience.

It was Disney who believed so fervently that turn-of-the-century America was the ideal home that he ordered a Main Street in every park he designed, even in Europe and Japan; it was Eisner who said, in connection with the ill-fated American history park in Virginia, that America "is the best of all possible places, [the] place that you are happy you are living in—and if you are not living there, you would love to be part of the American experience."

It was Disney who said, "The worst of us is not without innocence, though buried deeply it may be. In my work I try to reach and speak to that innocence . . . showing it that the human species, although happily ridiculous at times, is reaching for the stars." And Eisner who said, "My value is in the area of making sure that everything we do is ethical, moral, and creatively of the highest quality."

In some ways, Eisner forms the perfect complement to Disney, the yang to Walt's yin: Disney came from the nation's heartland with more pencil lead than money and built a world—really a universe—out of fantastic imagination and frontier-busting technology. Michael Eisner, who came from a world of wealth and cosmopolitan learning, revitalized the Disney Company by returning it to its filmmaking roots. And it is Eisner who is finally building the "community of tomorrow," the town called Celebration, not as a cool, futuristic Epcot, but as a real-life, neighborly minded Main Street, U.S.A.

"Call Me Michael"

One of the heavily promoted aspects of Disney corporate philosophy is that everybody, from the top to the bottom, is on a first-name basis. "He said, 'Call me Michael,'" a still somewhat awed employee said some months after meeting CEO Eisner. Although he's now a mature 60, "Mr. Eisner" might seem a little stiff for a guy who is 6'3" with a nose frequently compared to Howdy Doody's and a sheepish little bald spot in the middle of his rumpled hair. (*Washington Post* reporter William Powers once described him as "the man with the Tom Sawyer face and the sandpaper voice.")

Besides, this is the guy who added *All My Children* and *One Life to Live* to ABC's daytime programming and who worked on the warhorse *General Hospital*—which makes his creation of SoapNet, the 24-hour cable channel that rebroadcasts these ABC series and such older primetime series as *Falcon Crest* and *Dynasty* for nightowls, a kind of sentimental journey. He's the guy who invented *Happy Days* while stranded by a snowstorm in the Newark airport and who helped produce such box office smashes for Paramount as *Saturday Night Fever, Raiders of the Lost Ark, Grease, Ordinary People, Star Trek, An Officer and a Gentleman, Flashdance, Friday the 13th, 48 Hrs.,* and *Beverly Hills Cop*. He's the guy who had such faith in one childhood friend's judgment that when she mentioned a funny script nobody at United Artists wanted to produce, Eisner went right to the telephone and ordered Paramount to pick it up: it became *Airplane,* which cost $4 million and made $40 million. He's the guy who compared *Footloose* to *The Scarlet Letter* and quotes Plato in connection with the Disney Institute. He's the CEO who filmed a sequence for the Disney-MGM Studios Tour wearing a Mickey Mouse watch so that Mickey himself could flash a Michael Eisner watch. He's a guy who reportedly eats popcorn for breakfast. "Whatever he does," producer Larry Gordon once remarked, "he does with 100 percent gusto"—the most Disney-like characteristic of them all.

For Walt, both "magic kingdoms," his Hollywood studio and the theme park, were happy products of his own natural bent. His tinkering with multidimensional camera techniques made real animation possible; his hankering for a fantasy playground for his children produced a modern phenomenon.

Eisner's election to chairman of Walt's company was the result of years of preparation, "schooling," one might say, at three TV networks and a major movie studio. As the Magic Kingdom was to Walt Disney, so Hollywood was to Eisner—the symbol of our dreams, of what life never was really like and what it always should *seem* to be in our hearts. (Eisner opened the Disney-MGM Studios by calling it "the Hollywood that never was and always will be.") Besides, Eisner is a bona fide member of the Disney generation, a classic Baby Boomer who knows every cultural touchstone of the last 30 years and who had a hand in creating several of them himself. "My biggest break," he once told the *New York Times,* "was being born in 1942. When I was 21, that was the target audience for everything. When I was 35, the target audience was 35. I always felt and acted as though I was the audience."

While Walt had to sneak his candy money past his father, Eisner probably never even heard the phrase "penny candy" as a child. (In fact, while most of those famous sites re-created in It's a Small World and the World Showcase were only photos to the young Walt Disney, Eisner has visited many of them.) Eisner was raised on Manhattan's Park Avenue and summered in its Westchester County suburbs; he went to a famous Princeton prep, the Lawrenceville School. On his father's side, he was the descendant of a Bohemian émigré named Sigmund Eisner who became the manufacturer of uniforms for both the Boy Scouts and the U.S. Army; his mother was cofounder of the American Safety Razor company and wealthy in her own right. Although he was not a great scholar, he was encouraged to read widely as a youth, and he famously sprinkles his conversation with literary and artistic references; he's a fan of modern art and post-modern architecture.

Eisner started his career at NBC as a page, originally a summer job he got through family friends, the Sarnoffs, who owned a large chunk of NBC's parent, RCA. He moved to CBS to take a slot in children's programming, then shifted to ABC in 1966, where he became a protégé of executive Barry Diller. Eisner took over first Saturday morning programming and then prime time, where he launched such successful sitcoms as *Happy Days* and *Welcome Back, Kotter*. And when Diller became chairman of Paramount Pictures, he took Eisner with him as studio president.

"A Deep Sleep Fell Upon the Entire Castle"

The story of the reinvigoration of the Disney Company beginning in the mid-1980s might well be called The Great Movie Ride. It starts with a struggle over the spirit of the company, weaves through threats of buyouts and loss of creative control, and ends up with the company sailing into a beautiful sunset, but with a new king, Michael Eisner—a Hollywood pro rather than a Disney family member—at the helm.

Walt Disney World itself was an unquestionable success: even though the oil embargo of 1973 and the recession that followed struck hard at the entire region—the Orlando Chamber of Commerce actually organized a sort of fire sale that chopped 10% off the price of all local property—and Disney World had to lay off some employees, it managed to recover in record time. In January 1975, astronauts Scott Carpenter, Gordon Cooper, and Jim Irwin ceremoniously opened Space Mountain, which has remained one of the park's most popular attractions. A few months later the plans for Epcot were announced, prepping that park's potential audience.

Theme park revenues continued to climb, reaching $434 million by 1980 and jumping even higher after the opening of Epcot in 1982. Meanwhile, however, the movie division, the company's standard-bearer, was stalling. A dozen animators quit the company over what they said was loss of artistic control, a desertion that was to set the studio back for a decade. By the mid-1980s, the trouble was clearly serious.

Disney's films began taking huge losses at the box office, and rifts developed between old-line Disney loyalists such as Card Walker and Dick Nunis, who thought the company should continue to make the sort of family movies it always had; company director Roy E. Disney, Walt's nephew and head of animation; and Walt's son-in-law (and former football pro) Ron Miller, then president of Walt Disney Productions, who argued that the movie division must change with the times and, more importantly, with the audiences. Miller pushed hard enough to persuade the board to okay a more "adult" movie company, called Touchstone, to release films outside the family mode (although its first film, *Splash,* barely earned its PG rating). Miller even tried to hire Eisner, then president of Paramount Pictures, to rescue Disney, but Eisner refused, accurately concluding the company wasn't "culturally ready," meaning corporately ready, to break with tradition.

By 1984, the company was so weakened and disunited that it became the target of ornate and sometimes interrelated takeover attempts. Roy Disney himself, who had resigned from the board, launched one campaign. Greenmail master Saul Steinberg acquired about 12% of the Disney stock, which scared the board into bringing in the real estate–rich Bass brothers of Texas. Another famous greenmail artist, Irwin Jacobs, also had a chunk of stock in hand, which the Basses bought. Even notorious junk-bond specialists Michael Milken and Ivan Boesky put in bids.

It was an expensive battle for the Disney Company, the company Walt swore would never be sold or surrendered. It spent nearly $60 million to buy out Steinberg and took on half a billion dollars in new debt, outraging many of its stockholders. When the dust settled, the dispirited Miller was out; Roy E. Disney was back as head of the animation division; and two film-industry veterans, Eisner, who had resigned from Paramount just ten days earlier, and Frank Wells, vice-chairman of Warner Bros., had been named chairman and CEO, respectively. Eisner also brought along Jeffrey Katzenberg, who had been with him at Paramount, to take over as chairman of Disney's movie and TV division.

Roll Film, Roll

Eisner and Wells were opposites that attracted. Though they had similarly quick intelligence and impulsiveness, Wells was more disciplined and steady: Despite his prep school background, Eisner attended an unremarkable Ohio college (Dennison); Wells was a former Rhodes scholar and Stanford Law graduate. Eisner slouched; Wells had impeccable carriage. Eisner's suits were custom-made but often a little askew; Wells would wear denim shirts on informal occasions, but they were always starched and immaculate. One of the few characteristics they shared was the ability to balance professional and personal ambitions (and a sense of fun): Wells had been president of Warner Bros. until he semi-retired to try climbing the highest mountains on each continent in the world. He and his partners nearly succeeded, in fact, but they failed twice to top Mount Everest.

But Eisner and Wells came to the Disney Company with a single purpose—to regild the studio's tarnished image. First, they assembled a group of stars, something like the old MGM studio system, by signing Robin Williams and Bette Midler, among others, to multimovie contracts. This resulted in a string of broad-audience successes for Touchstone Pictures, including *Down and Out in Beverly Hills* (the company's first R-rated film), *The Color of Money, Dead Poet's Society, Good Morning Vietnam, Big Business, Beaches, Pretty Woman, Father of the Bride, The Nightmare Before Christmas, Three Men and a Baby* (Eisner wandered into the French original, *Trois Hommes et un Couffin,* when he saw people on the Champs Elysées lining up to get in), *Sister Act,* and *What's Love Got to Do with It?* Eisner, Wells, and Katzenberg immediately pushed film production schedules from 4 to 14 films a year—and then went further by establishing a third film outlet called Hollywood Pictures

Disney also moved more aggressively into television, not only launching the Disney cable channel but commissioning original Touchstone series, which included such high-grossing hits as Tim Allen's *Home Improvement* and *The Golden Girls.* To further cash in on such Disney and ABC stars as Tim Allen and Jeff Foxworthy, Eisner had Disney's Hyperion Books publish their comic autobiographies, both best-sellers.

Eisner had other good ideas for raising money. He ordered *Pinocchio* to be released on videocassette well ahead of its regular theatrical re-release schedule (so a new audience would have time to be born), and netted more than $12 million. He discovered that the nearly 500 cartoons and three decades of *Wonderful World of Disney* episodes in the vaults had never been sold to syndication—an oversight he immediately corrected, raising $40 million in a single month in 1985. And, in what sounds like the most obvious of decisions, he ordered company publicity staffers to come up with an advertising campaign for the theme parks, the first promotion for the parks in the company's history. Attendance immediately jumped 10%.

The Disney Company had sniffed out the merchandising possibilities of its shows early, and the mouse ears and Davy Crockett coonskin caps were legends of the business. But merchandising had never been a major concern. Coming from the *Star Trek* and *Happy Days* franchises, Eisner was far more merchandise-savvy than his predecessors. He was intrigued by the possibilities not merely of T-shirts and ears, but of collectible figurines and limited-reproduction cels and cloned trees. On his watch (pun intended), Disney merchandise has become one of the most profitable arms of the company. In 1995 more than $15 billion worth of Disney merchandise was sold around the world. A single cel from *Pocahontas* went at a Sotheby's auction for close to $21,000.

Wells and Eisner also put plans for movie studio–style attractions on the front burner. Not only was this project a natural match—most of the attractions at the Disney-MGM Studios salute, steal from, or restage movie hits from the company—but there were rumors that Universal Studios was planning to open a similar attraction only a few miles away from Disney World. Universal's parent company, MCA, was particularly bitter when the Disney-MGM Studios theme park was announced, since the Bass brothers, who rode into the Disney Company as white knights to stop the greenmail takeover attempts (and wound up with a 25% stake as prize), had been approached by MCA about investing in just such a project.

And they decided to broaden Disney's movie-audience appeal—just as Walt had done, using Buena Vista to release nature films when the market for animated films seemed to have dried up. Hollywood Pictures, which debuted with

ne Disney's conduit to the mass market;
been *Crimson Tide, While You Were Sleep-*
, *The Rock,* and *Mr. Holland's Opus.*
ied the teen and young-adult label, but it
l the romantic mid-adult market too: over
ed *The Waterboy, Holy Man, He Got Game,*
Rushmore, Krippendorf's Tribe, 10 Things I
Other Sister (an update of Shakespeare's
, *Con Air, High Fidelity, Gone in 60 Sec-*
or (based on a novel by Michael "Jurassic
anghai Noon, Mission to Mars (once the
attraction in early Tomorrowland), and
released some "women's" films, such as
tty-baby version of the Dalai Lama's story;
vith Robert Redford; and *Beloved*—which,
of Oprah book club backing, should have
mong middle age women, but which fell
astonishingly flat.

The most daring of the sub-studios, Miramax, begun as Disney's intro into the hip/indie/European market, released such relatively daring films as *Priest, Unzipped,* and *Pulp Fiction.* The former two films contributed to church groups' denunciation of the company's degenerating values, and a few years later led Disney to withdraw backing for another potentially controversial film called *Dogma. Pulp Fiction* director Quentin Tarantino was offered a special "vanity film" subdivision called Rolling Thunder, and the company, wanting to put even more distance between itself and the underage-sex film *Kids,* distributed that movie via the once-and-perhaps-future Excalibur Films.

Miramax became the more "literary" label: it released such films as *Emma,* in the wake of the Jane Austin craze; the Cinderella-style *She's All That, The English Patient,* and the super-hit *Shakespeare in Love* (a co-production with Paramount), as well as the surprise hit *Life Is Beautiful.* It also remained the primary indie-style label, releasing *Rounders, A Civil Action, Playing By Heart,* and *Celebrity.* And longtime Disney stalwart Robin Williams was finally rewarded with an Academy Award for his role in the hit *Good Will Hunting.* Miramax was one of the most glittering proofs of Eisner's seeming Midas touch: started for $80 million in 1993, it was generating annual profits of $125 million only five years later.

Miramax also owns the Dimension Films division, which specializes in teen-terror flicks such as *Scary Movie, Scream,* and *Spy Kids* (and their numerous sequels), *Halloween H20, The Legend of Drunken Master,* and a host of straight-to-video knockoffs.

But it was the status label, the Walt Disney Films name itself, that Eisner and Wells were most determined to revive, and where in 1989 they hit the jackpot with *The Little Mermaid,* which announced the renaissance of Disney animation and grossed $80 million. Other Disney hits of the 1990s included *Aladdin* (which grossed $200 million and spun off a TV series), *Pocahontas, Dick Tracy, Who Framed Roger Rabbit?* (which grossed $150 million), *Honey, I Shrunk the Kids, The Hunchback of Notre Dame, Mulan* (which made $115 million in the U.S. alone), and *The Lion King* (which grossed $1 billion). All these films have been recycled as stage shows, live-action parades, rides, and/or souvenir merchandise at Disney World; this ensures their audiences are continually excited about visiting the park. Even the stage set from the new, non-animated *101 Dalmations* built outside London had to be reassembled at Walt Disney World. The stage required two 42-ton shipping containers and a special 20-ton cradle for Cruella's car.

Disney's animated features of the 1990s began to display Eisner's shrewd use of "synergy"—movies that reflected Disney's TV shows, and vice versa— as well as his equally market-savvy collaborations with pop and rock superstars whose soundtrack contributions could be counted on to boost sales. (Release of the live-action *Mighty Ducks,* about a kids' hockey team and its bad-boy coach, actually predated the creation of the NHL team by a year, but you get the idea.) These films included *Doug's First Movie,* based on the successful animated TV show; the phenomenally profitable *Lion King,* whose Elton John–Tim Rice score not only inspired a Broadway show but also led the musical team to produce Disney's modern-Broadway update of the opera *Aida;* and the long-waited *Tarzan,* with a Phil Collins soundtrack and skateboard-inspired choreography. (Weirdly, at the same time Disney released *Tarzan,* the traditional king of the apes story, its sibling studio Touchstone was releasing *Instinct,* starring Anthony Hopkins as a man who lives so long with the great apes that he, well, goes ape and kills a poacher.)

The Dinosaur attraction at Animal Kingdom was always presumed to be a sort of 3-D trailer for *Dinosaur,* which emerged from its shell in 2000. Well in advance of the rerelease of *Fantasia* and the IMAX-formatted *Fantasia 2000,* Disney-MGM Studios unveiled its daily curtain-closer, the ornate laser-fireworks *Fantasmic!* based on the Sorcerer's Apprentice segment. And there are reportedly features in development based on three of Disney World's most enduring attractions, *Pirates of the Caribbean,* the *Haunted Mansion,* and the *Country Bears Jamboree.*

Disney's more traditional family films also stuck close to home, with such similarly in-the-family releases as a remake of *The Parent Trap, Mighty Joe Young* (another great-ape fable, though not so successful), live-action versions of *101* (and *102*) *Dalmations,* and *I'll Be Home for Christmas,* starring teen heartthrob Jonathan Taylor Thomas of *Home Improvement,* one of Touchstone TV's great moneymakers.

Together, these companies fulfilled their mission to make Disney a name to be reckoned with in the film industry again. By the end of 1998, when it posted gross domestic returns of $1.1 billion, Disney had ruled as Hollywood's top money maker four out of five years. *Armageddon,* also released in 1998, made $554 million; *The Sixth Sense* earned $530 million in 1999. In fact, Disney biz was so big that film executives decided to combine the Hollywood, Touchstone, and Disney labels under the organizational (and nostalgic) name Buena Vista Pictures, saying the company had so many irons in the fire that it would have to cut its moviemaking schedule from 40 films a year to a mere 20.

Intriguingly, Eisner and his colleagues also began experimenting with releasing independent-style adult and even mature-audience films under the original Disney rubric at the same time as it chugged ahead with the animated works—perhaps thinking that they could use the Disney name to draw the older crowds they were luring to the parks in increasing numbers. At the 1999 Cannes Film Festival, Disney was represented by an astonishing three films, one directed by Spike Lee,

(Summer of Sam, set in the Bronx during the time of the Son of Sam killings*), The Straight Story,* an unusually sweet film by David *(Blue Velvet, Twin Peaks)* Lynch, and the third, a drama called *Cradle Will Rock,* by Tim Robbins, who previously directed *Dead Man Walking.*

Disney also backed *O Brother, Where Art Thou?,* an unlikely-sounding Depression-era resetting of *Ulysses* with an period soundtrack, from the Coen brothers, who made such offbeat hits as *Fargo,* and such even more offbeat films as *The Big Lebowski:* it not only became a hit, its soundtrack topped both critics' lists and sales charts despite a total absence of radio play. (Unfortunately, Disney had not thought to lock up the recording rights.)

A Very Un-Merry Birthday

Nevertheless, at the turn of the century, and just as Disney geared up to celebrate the centennial of Walt Disney's Birth, the studio seemed to be slipping from the gold standard to something more alloyed. A string of animated features, including *Dinosaur, The Emperor's New Groove,* and *Atlantis,* inspired only lukewarm box office returns. *Beloved* with Oprah Winfrey cost about $60 million to make and earned perhaps $10 million; and the remake of *Mighty Joe Young* reportedly cost $100 million and earned only two-thirds of that. The blockbuster-sized live-action *Pearl Harbor,* featuring *Titanic*-style special effects, did gross $430 million worldwide, but that still fell a little short of what it would have had to make to lift Disney stock. (It came in at $130 million, but only after many of its stars and crew agreed to take salary cuts in favor of expected profit-sharing.)

Edgier productions such as *The Shipping News* and *The Royal Tennenbaums* similarly faded quickly; and although *The Rookie,* based on a suitably inspiring true story of a 37-year-old baseball pitcher (sort of the Natural meets the Mighty Ducks in midlife crisis), did fairly well, *Gangs of New York,* a 1920s-period film directed by Martin Scorcese and starring *Titanic* idol Leonardo di Caprio and scheduled for 2002, was pushed off at least until 2003.

Better news—and a likely indication of Eisner's direction in the future—is the Cuba Gooding family movie *Snow Dogs,* which cost about $30 million to make and which grossed more than $80 million. The *Peter Pan* sequel *Return to Never-Land* was made by Disney animators in Australia for $20 million, for about a $10 million profit—a modest budget success, but again likely bound for video resurrection.

The one remaining source of apparently guaranteed box-office gold is Disney's partnership with Pixar, the computer-animation film company founded by Apple Computers' cofounder Steve Jobs. Not surprisingly, the studio that invented feature animation was not content to depend on traditional cartooning techniques—especially as several other studios began to issue feature-length animated films.

In 1996, the studios released *Toy Story,* and in 1998, *A Bug's Life,* which became two of Disney's most successful animated films and sources of merchandising spin-offs (as well as inspiration for Disney World attractions): *A Bug's Life,* for example, grossed $120 million in the United States alone; *Toy Story II* doubled that figure. And the fourth Disney-Pixar release, *Monsters, Inc.,* had the sixth-best opening in movie history, earning $62.5 million its first weekend (eventually climbing to $500 million worldwide).

But even the Disney-Pixar partnership was a little strained by the tight financial times; Disney's original financial backing for Pixar had come at the price of a five-feature deal, with Disney, as the greater risk-taker, also getting most of the profits. By 2001, the two companies were at odds over whether a third *Toy Story* film, which Disney was eager to release, would count as the fifth film, which would allow Pixar to renegotiated its deal. Disney executives, however, were determined to keep *TSIII* out of the package. Eisner's uncharacteristically tactless criticism of computers' CD-burning capabilities further irked Jobs. After Disney threw a lavish 15th birthday party for Pixar at the Bel-Air Country Club, however, the two studios mended fences and announced the last two titles would be *The Incredibles* and *Finding Nemo*—another salute to an old Disney hit, *20,000 Leagues Under the Sea.* Nevertheless, this wrangle, though not widely publicized, was pointed to by some of Eisner's critics as another example of his often rocky business relationships (see below).

Animation is Job One at Disney for a very good reason: it's highly profitable. Six of the top-selling videos of 1998 were

Disney's, including *Lion King II: Simba's Pride, Peter Pan, The Little Mermaid,* and *Hercules.* Sequels produced intentionally as videos are even more profitable, and the new DVD market has allowed some of the most popular titles a third life, sometimes in the same family. Even a film that is only a moderate success, such as *The Parent Trap* remake, is likely to earn $50 million in later video sales. These films can be recycled through the whole system of Disney outlets: the cartoon channel, *Wonderful World of Disney,* the Disney Channel, and its international spin-offs. And the videos themselves can be padded with advertisements and commercials for Disney World, Disney's cruise line, memorabilia, other videos, etc.

One media analyst explained it to the *New York Times* this way: "If Disney invests $10 in a live-action film, they are lucky if they can return $12 that they can keep. For an animated film, they expect to keep at least $25 on a $10 investment," thanks to soundtrack, video, and merchandising sales. No wonder Disney has announced it will pull back on adult-fare live-action and concentrate again on Disney-brand entertainment.

Eisner has even taken the movies a step further by bringing the cartoons to life. In order to put *Beauty and the Beast* on stage, Disney bought and renovated the Palace Theater near Times Square as a family-style theater, as well as the glorious old El Capitan Theatre in Los Angeles. The production budget was an estimated $14 million, and the computer set-up alone cost another $6 million. Putting on the musical cost $400,000 every week, but by the summer of 1996 there were simultaneous productions running in New York, Los Angeles, Washington, D.C., Toronto, Vienna, Tokyo, Osaka, and Melbourne. And the half-live, half-puppet *Lion King* show is sold out for years to come.

Hopes are currently focussed on a full-length animated feature (perhaps designed to follow on the heels of the 20th anniversary rerelease of *E.T.: The Extraterrestrial*) called *Lilo and Stitch,* about a girl on holiday in Hawaii who befriends an alien. It's expected to do so well that there are already rumors the *Alien Encounter* ride will be retooled to fit the new film.

The Wonderful World of Color

Television has always been a major player in the Disney empire, and it remains perhaps even more essential today. The Capital

Cities/ABC deal—the second largest commercial merger in U.S. history, behind only the notorious $25 billion buyout of RJR Nabisco in 1989—brought Disney not only the widely profitable ESPN but substantial stakes in the Arts & Entertainment (A&E) channel (which also includes the prestigious History Channel), the E! Entertainment network, and Lifetime cable, all of which have between 75 million and 85 million subscribers; several magazine groups, including the publishers of *W* and *Women's Wear Daily;* and, in a nostalgic coincidence that would have pleased Walt himself, a group of newspapers, including the *Kansas City Star.*

Disney also owns the Disney Channel, Disney Toon, Soap-Net (which costs virtually nothing to operate and which has 18 million subscribers), and in 2001 purchased the Fox Family Channel for $5.2 billion, renaming it the Disney Family Channel. As much as one-fourth of the Family Channel's programming will be rebroadcast from ABC—its New Year's Day schedule was a 24-hour *Alias* marathon—and the $80 million check ABC handed Warner Bros. for the broadcast rights to *Harry Potter: The Sorcerer's Stone* also covers its cable airing. Disney also has cable subscribers in a dozen countries around the world, and agreements to launch another half-dozen.

Animation is top dog here, as well; as many as 200 cartoon projects are estimated to be in some stage of development at a time, either for broadcast, cable or possible video. The entire Saturday morning ABC lineup serves as a tie-in to other Disney projects (synergy again). And the company's animators provide additional animated series for the UPN network or syndicators.

Although it is not producing many of its own series, except for the Saturday night *Wonderful World of Disney,* which combines rebroadcasts of Disney favorites with remakes and some new TV movies, "family values" is still a heavy component, even when there is some adult material (the daytime sops, *Felicity,* etc.). Eisner is firmly opposed to the more flagrant forms of "reality TV," and shortly after acquiring ABC, he axed the Jerry Springer-style *Jenny Jones Show.* "There are two ways to make money in entertainment, the high road or the low road," Eisner told Fortune magazine. "The low road is a road I don't choose to be on."

However, Disney's more visible television operations are struggling. In 1995, when Disney bought ABC, the network was ranked No. 1, with such successful series as *Roseanne, Home Improvement,* and *NYPD Blue.* A few years later, it had fallen to third (on one famous occasion, it actually came in fifth, behind not only NBC and CBS but also WB and UPN programming). Its primetime audience fell another 24% in the 2001–2002 season, forcing ABC to return some advertising payments or offer addition ad spots to compensate its clients. And as viewer numbers fell, so did the rates ABC was able to charge; early in 2002, Merrill-Lynch estimated the network's losses for the year would reach $500 million.

Worse, the network seemed to have lost its sense of the popular culture—the very gut-feeling factor Eisner had always claimed was his strongest point. ABC's much-publicized attempt to lure late-night talk show host David Letterman away from CBS to replace the prestigious but less advertiser-attractive news show *Nightline* with Ted Koppel (and its subsequent kiss-and-makeup contract with Koppel) was a PR nightmare, particularly after Letterman not so subtly criticized ABC for its willingness to dump *Nightline.* When one of the myriad programming chiefs who came and went at ABC in the late 1990s didn't particularly care for a police procedural series developed at Touchstone Television, the studio sold off its rights; *CSI: Crime Scene Investigation* became a hit for CBS instead. And the comet-like career of *Who Wants to Be a Millionaire,* which pulled in a record profit of $518 million in 2000, was expanded to four nights a week, wearing out its welcome, and flamed out only a year later, without its windfall having been used to develop new programs.

Nevertheless, as visible as ABC's troubles are, they represent only a fragment of the financial Disney World, about 5% of operating income. ABC stations continue to dominate local ratings, and the network comes in second to NBC in evening news slots. (ABC owns 10 television and 53 radio stations.) The daytime programming has been outdrawing its competition for 25 years—since Eisner's time. The popularity of *Felicity, My Wife and Kids* (Touchstone's first entry into the black urban-comedy market), and *Alias* in 2001 gave the company renewed status. And Robert Iger, who ran ABC for six years before being named president of the Walt Disney Co., pledged to refocus his attention on the network's performance and predicted a revived ABC could add as much as $10 a share to the price of Disney stock.

"I Can't Wait to Be King"

If Walt was worried about anybody giving away the store, he's happy now: Michael Eisner has been, even given the recent downturn, the best thing to happen to Disney Enterprises since Uncle Walt himself. Charismatic and successful, Eisner never misses a trick—and plays most of them close to the vest. In fact, employees say the corporation declined one of the Commerce Department's Malcolm Baldridge Awards for Excellence because the panel would have had to go over too many figures that Eisner preferred to keep private.

Eisner is often referred to as the highest-paid CEO in America, although his actual salary is only $750,000; his contract was designed with lavish stock options and bonuses based on stock performance. In December 1992, a day before new tax regulations were to take effect, he cashed in some of his stock options worth more than $200 million and sold them for a $127 million profit. In fiscal 1994 he made about $10.6 million in salary, bonuses, and stock awards. And in fiscal 1995 he went home with $15.5 million: $750,000 in straight salary, plus an $8 million bonus geared to the company's stock performance and another $6.8 million in stock options. Even in fiscal 1998, which Eisner himself called a "flat year" and in which his "bonus" was halved to a mere $5 million, he quietly sold another $560 million worth of stock; he exercised another $50 million in 1999. Altogether, Eisner made an estimated $1 billion in his first 15 years at Disney, easily enough to boost him into Forbes' 500, albeit only in the high 300s. (He has taken only one bonus since then.)

He thinks big for Disney, as well. After Disney bought Capital Cities/ABC in August 1995, Eisner enjoyed telling network stars that it was the price—more than $19 billion—that made it attractive. He also said that Disney needed to invest so much money to balance its profits that it turned down the CBS network, offered at a mere $5.5 billion, as "too cheap," an idea that might have made him squirm a few years later.

Executives, talent agents, producers, and financiers all famously considered Eisner to have an astonishing instinct for entertainment. Many of his colleagues staked their careers on his: nearly two dozen Paramount employees followed him to Disney. Former Disney chief financial officer Stephen Bollenbach, now at Hilton Hotels, told *The New Yorker* that Eisner has "an uncanny ability to look at a project, whether it's a film or an animated feature or a theme-park ride, and after a hundred really smart people have screened it he will invariably come in and ask the simplest, smartest question." And Frank Wells, who might have had the top job himself in 1994, reportedly told Disney board members to choose Eisner over himself or former 20th Century Fox chairman Dennis Stanfill, another candidate, because "good creative judgment is unique, even in this town."

Eisner is not, however, universally admired. His very creativity, which at times takes on a loose cannon approach, and his populist instincts have made some more conservative Hollywood insiders nervous. "If he weren't Michael Eisner, you'd think this guy was a lunatic," a safely anonymous studio executive told a reporter. Among his more famous proposals that never made it off the drawing board are a 45-story hotel in the shape of Mickey Mouse and a Winnebago journey across America with his family to get in touch with the people—something like the Clinton/Gore caravan of 1991. In the same interview during which he praised Eisner's instincts, Bollenbach also said Eisner micromanages "to a fault," and "the fault is that it physically drains him"— a prophetic remark, as it turned out.

Within ten years of their "coup," Eisner, Wells, Katzenberg, and Co. had transformed Disney, which had less than $1.5 billion in revenue in 1984 and not many promising projects on the horizon, into a company with $10 billion in revenues and an estimated net worth five times that. The value of Disney stock rose by more than 1,000% in the same ten years.

Then came a series of escalating corporate crises, beginning in April 1994 with Wells's death in a helicopter crash. Only a few months later, Eisner, who was deeply affected by his partner's loss and seemingly ever more obsessed with detail, was felled by chest pains and underwent emergency heart surgery.

Nevertheless, Eisner refused to promote Disney Studios chief Jeffrey Katzenberg to Wells's CEO slot—reneging, according to Katzenberg, on a promise to do so—so Katzenberg walked out.

(Eisner couldn't have been too surprised: the reason Katzenberg resigned from Paramount was that he had been passed over as chairman.) Published reports estimated that Katzenberg's decision to quit without exercising one more year's options cost him $100 million. Katzenberg also persuaded several other key officials, including TV chief Rich Frank, and another handful of animators to go with him.

In a blaze of pique and publicity, Katzenberg joined music tycoon David Geffen and superstar movie director Steven Spielberg in organizing the DreamWorks SKG studio. As soon as DreamWorks went public, Katzenberg, Spielberg, and Geffen each realized paper profits of $567 million. Nevertheless, his pride wounded, Katzenberg sued the Disney Company for $100 million, claiming the company owed him that much for his work on *Lion King, Aladdin,* and so on. In the ten years he ran the studio, its profits leaped from $244 million to a staggering $4.8 billion, and a clause in his contract said he was entitled to a 2% cut of those profits. Disney attorneys argued that he had forfeited his percentage when he resigned. Eventually Disney agreed to pay Katzenberg a hefty (though unspecified) settlement, but the suit continued, and after a particularly nasty public trial, in which it was revealed that Eisner had commented, "I think I hate that little midget," the court agreed that the five-foot-four Katzenberg was indeed owed substantially more—by some estimates topping $500 million.

For a while after Katzenberg resigned, Eisner again tried to go it alone, naming himself CEO as well as chairman. Eventually, he hired super-agent Michael Ovitz, head of Creative Artists Agency and a longtime friend, as president of the company. But even that soured almost immediately: Only months after Ovitz's hiring, the *New Yorker's* Ken Auletta quoted a friend of both men who said that Eisner complained, "You know, I knew and vacationed with and dined with Michael Ovitz for 25 years, but I didn't know him at all. That's the mistake I made when I brought him in here. He doesn't know how business operates." After only 14 months on the job, Ovitz resigned, taking with him a cool $39 million in cash and $60 million-plus in stock options as severance pay—about $7 million per month worked. (At the same time, Eisner signed a contract to stay on through

September 2006, adding an additional 8 million stock options worth approximately $456 million to his portfolio.)

One of Michael Ovitz's first moves when he joined Disney was to hire hot young prospect Jamie Tarses, the 32-year-old creator of *Friends* and *Frasier,* away from NBC to head ABC Entertainment, a move that involved spreading rumors of sexual harassment against an NBC executive to help break her contract. Her unsurprising efforts to bring ABC into the young-market mainstream were unsuccessful and confusing, and she left, somewhat acrimoniously, after only a couple of years. For a time there were co-chairmen, which only made matters more confusing.

Altogether, since 1997, Disney has lost one president, two studio chiefs, two CFOs, and three ABC heads. ABC Entertainment, which manages the network's prime-time schedule, has had six management teams in the last six years. (There are also many who have been with Disney for more than a decade.) Both insiders and outside analysts have said that the personnel upheavals are at least in part a matter of corporate culture clash— Eisner's hands-on, top-down management style vs. ABC's more decentralized setup. One headhunter blamed Disney for not doing enough to retain top executives. "There was a certain arrogance and hubris attendant to the success," he told Fortune magazine. "Now it's compounded by a certain defensiveness."

However, the installation of former ABC, Inc. president Iger as Disney Co. president has inspired many stock analysts to predict a turnaround in company fortunes. (Iger himself has said he spent too much time managing the merger of Disney and ABC rather than managing the companies themselves.) Most recently, Eisner has hired Fred Silverman, who has served as president of all three major networks, as a consultant; and promoted Susan Lyne, a former journalist and head of ABC's movies/miniseries division, to head of ABC Entertainment, actions that appear to have increased stability. Eisner has personally taken charge of the movie studio, despite naming a longtime aide to the nominal chairmanship.

According to a story by Robert Sam Anson in *Los Angeles* magazine, these often bitter partings are more characteristic than Eisner's long and close relationship with Frank Wells. As Anson noted, many other Hollywood executives had once been close friends of Eisner, then become estranged—and in a few cases, become friends again. Geffen, now an Eisner critic because of the Katzenberg break, previously had been an admirer and had discussed partnerships and mergers with Eisner several times over the years. Eisner even explored the idea of Disney's buying Geffen Records for $400 million, but the deal was never consummated, and Geffen eventually sold out to MCA. Steven Spielberg, the third member of the DreamWorks team, had also worked with Eisner repeatedly, both at Paramount *(Raiders of the Lost Ark)* and Disney *(Who Framed Roger Rabbit?)*.

Barry Diller, Eisner's mentor at ABC and later Paramount Pictures, was one of Eisner's biggest boosters when he first took over Disney. Now CEO of USA Network and its subsidiaries, Expedia and Home Shopping Network (other lucrative and no doubt competitively "synergistic" outlets), Diller is no longer speaking to him. MCA chairman Sid Sheinberg has been blunt in his criticism of what he considers Eisner's conning of the media.

Several insiders—some eventually hired by Disney or ABC and some not—have been reported to feel manipulated or insulted by clumsy recruiting and corporate in-fighting. An unauthorized 2000 biography by sometime *Variety* and *Washington Post* reporter Kim Masters, called *The Keys to the Kingdom: How Michael Eisner Lost His Grip* (which, Masters charged, Eisner attempted to squash), quoted many of these adversaries, although Frank Wells' widow rather pointedly declined to participate. And Miramax founders Robert and Harvey Weinstein have been left free to steer their company as they choose.

Eisner also led Disney into some very visible and rancorous fights with Time-Warner over ABC cable rights (at one point, cable subscribers in New York were unable to watch ABC), and he opposed the AOL–Time Warner merger on the grounds that it gave one company too many "vertical" tie-ins, something of a contraction, considering Disney's many acquisitions.

The rivalry between Universal and Disney, who have spent much of the last decade attempting to one-up each other's theme parks in California and Florida, is quite sharp. Universal employees, even artists, who formerly worked on Disney projects are afraid to display any memorabilia for fear of retribution. At the *Jaws* ride in Universal Studios Florida, only a few minutes from Walt Disney World, there is a half-eaten boat floating in the water; near the water is a Mickey Mouse–ears hat. At Universal's Hollywood park, the wrecked boat is in the *Jurassic Park* ride, and the Mickey Mouse hat has the name "Michael" on it.

The bad feeling has also trickled down throughout the animation community, which no longer openly exchanges ideas and projects. One of the ways Katzenberg attempted revenge was to hire away many of Disney's best artists, launching a salary war as well as a commercial one. DreamWorks released its first animated feature, *Antz,* just before Disney got *A Bug's Life* into theaters. The only problem with that, according to ex-Apple chief and Pixar Animation founder Steve Jobs, was that Katzenberg "knew all about *Bug's* the day he left Disney. We pitched it to him." (Pixar, for its part, hired away Disney animator/director John Lassiter, who has worked on most of the joint projects.)

More pointedly, Dreamworks' hit *Shrek* struck a number of sly anti-Disney notes, though the satire was fairly broadly applied. One particularly famous slap involves a scene where the princess is singing along with a bluebird, a la *Snow White,* only in the *Shrek* version she trills up so high that the bird, puffing fatter and whistling harder to keep up, finally explodes.

The Greatest Shows on Earth

In some ways, the late 1990s drop in profits might have been foreseen. Michael Eisner has lived up to Walt's original Disney World rule: He has never built anything on a small scale. Reading about Disney projects can be like reading the federal budget: the zeroes tend to lose their impact. The $19.5 billion purchase of Capital Cities/ABC is far and away the largest, outside the $80 billion value of Disney itself. But as the entertainment conglomerate's interests broadened, so did its outlays. Disney paid more than $10 billion to get the broadcast rights for NFL and college football, $4.5 million on behalf of ESPN alone (an offer that raised the eyebrows and concerns of consumer advocates and cable operators, who say constantly escalating broadcasting contracts are ultimately passed along to viewers). ABC also cornered the football bowls market, paying $525 million over seven years to air the four name games of the new national collegiate championship series—the Rose, Sugar, Orange, and Fiesta Bowls.

As pointed out in "Pleasure World," the company has spent billions on sports acquisitions, franchise bids, and facilities in recent years. And such gifts just keep on giving, so to speak: aside from simply buying into major league baseball and hockey, for example, Disney entered the free-agent market with a bang, paying first basemen Mo Vaughn $80 million over six years to join the Angels (though he's since moved on to the Mets) and giving Mighty Duck Teemu Selanne nearly $20 million for two years (and he's since moved to the San Jose Sharks).

In order to bolster its various websites and to take advantage of the network browsing habit learned by Yahoo!, Netscape, and other Internet portals, Disney paid the equivalent of $90 million plus its ownership of Starwave Corp. for 43% of Infoseek, and then used it to help launch the Go network.

Disney-MGM Studios, which is about the same size as the Magic Kingdom (with somewhat less concentrated fantasy), cost a relatively modest $300 million, but then it had only about half the number of attractions it has today. The 1994–1995 renovation of Tomorrowland alone cost $100 million. The entire Disneyland in Anaheim is undergoing significant expansion and renovation. And the huge Animal Kingdom park, originally expected to cost $760 million, may end up costing close to a billion dollars—a stunning figure that is the largest single budget in Disney history. (Although, if the American history theme park outside Washington, D.C., had passed muster, it would have cost at least $650 million.)

The cost of just one individual attraction can be mind-boggling. The 17-minute *Captain EO* 3-D attraction that involved Michael Jackson, Frances Ford Coppola, and George Lucas and was the predecessor to *Honey, I Shrunk the Audience* cost $17 million, and that was considered extravagant in 1986. *The Twilight Zone* Tower of Terror, added in 1994, ate up $95 million, not counting its various facelifts. And *Alien Encounter,* first opened in 1995, cost about $60 million. In the "sponsorship" era, figures are fuzzier, but Test Track cost GM a rumored $30 million for its part alone.

Other late 1990s projects included the renovation and expansion of the Disney Village Marketplace, which also included the construction of Disney's West Side; Disney's Wide World of Sports, which cost an estimated $100 million; the $235 million Coronado Springs Resort and convention center; and the cruise ship line, plus the California Adventure park adjoining Disneyland. Disney even bought a deserted island in the Bahamas to use as a stopover for its cruises. The town of Celebration (see the next section) cost $2.5 billion. Currently on the drawing board are a Mediterranean-themed resort, another Vacation Club resort adjoining the Wilderness Lodge (and possibly a BoardWalk-like entertainment center between them), a monorail connecting Epcot and the MGM Studios, and the currently stalled budget family resort called Pop Century.

But as the company got bigger, it had more places for money to drain out of. ABC's proposed round-the-clock cable news service, designed to go head-to-head with CNN's, was abandoned when projections suggested heavy start-up costs (losses of as much as $400 million in its first four years) and falling audience projections. And Disney's various online services were similarly expensive: between April 1997 and June 1998, ABC News.com lost $21.5 million on revenue of $9.1 million, ESPN.com lost $7.2 million on revenue of $21.5 million, and Infoseek (later Go.com) had an operating loss of $7.6 million for just the first nine months of 1998.

The merchandise stores, which at one point were popping up in every major shopping mall in the country (and 11 foreign countries) and bringing in 250 million customers a year, gradually lost focus (or taste, some critics said) and business. At one point, a group of stockholders even filed suit against the Disney board of directors for approving Ovitz's platinum parachute.

The huge cost of some of its pictures caused Eisner to move the company more toward co-financing live films, selling off the foreign rights to some films (such as Michael Crichton's *The 13th Warrior*) producing others abroad, and joining forces with other corporations such as Sony Pictures on future projects. And the post-9/11 crash in air travel and tourism in general, while obviously not Eisner's fault, squeezed stock prices even tighter, to less than $20 a share—just about where it was after the costly acquisition of ABC. By early 2002, the company's market capitalization had dropped to $50 billion.

Like many companies, Disney took indirect hits from the stock market recession as well. The influential investor Warren Buffett sold most of Berkshire-Hathaway's Disney holdings in 1999. Texas billionaire Sid Bass, who had helped Eisner financially by purchasing large blocks of stock (and therefore gained influence on executive hirings) during the 1984 contest, was embarrassingly caught selling Disney stock on margin after September 11 and had to liquidate 135 million shares. Eisner has said he tried to interest Buffett in buying some of them, but that Buffett felt his company was too strapped by the terrorist attacks' drain on its insurance properties. Eisner also gave Bass some social cover by saying his old ally had warned him even before September 11 that he was having cash trouble, and he took a little advantage of the Bass stock's low price by buying back 50 million shares. Recessionary ad revenues were also blamed for the demise of *Talk* magazine, the ambitious but sometimes catty cultural monthly launched jointly by Hearst and Disney.

However, the company has made several crucial moves that have impressed financial analysts. More than 4,000 jobs have been cut, most from Internet operations which have been drastically cut back and are expected to be back in the black in 2002; the Go.com portal has been closed entirely. The company is closing approximately a third of the 600 or so Disney merchandise stores and, having brought in former Nike CEO Andrew Mooney as division president, is moving toward more adult designs, less obtrusive logos, and more upscale store decor, as well as signing distribution deals with major retailers including J.C. Penney. (We even noticed a Mickey Mouse waffle iron for sale at Sears.)

The decision to alter film production partnership deals and film budgets is believed to be saving $600 million a year. The company's home video and burgeoning DVD distribution operations are highly profitable. It also produces animated and syndicated programming for UPN and foreign markets.

Construction of the Mediterranean-theme resort and the Pop Century hotels at Walt Disney World has been delayed, as has the reopening of the renovated Port Orleans; however, the Villas at Wilderness Lodge and Villas at Beach Club, both actually timeshare condos, will open on schedule. Another sort of frequent-visitors reward program called Club Disney and easier Internet booking on the way. And a newly-acquired children's entertainment company called Baby Einstein is being touted as the next Miramax.

Despite the closing of so many smaller and less-profitable sites, the elaborate Disney Store on Fifth Avenue in New York, with its lavish display of merchandise and its on-site vacation booking office for the resorts, and its sibling in Times Square, are both showcases of the company's strongest inventory. More Disney memorabilia is available through direct mail or galleries specializing in animation cels (and authorized reproductions thereof).

Disney also has a ten-year deal with McDonald's to open 18,700 joint theme restaurants around the world, with options for even more. There are now several Big Macs in the World, one in the Marketplace, one near the All-Star Sports resort (which looks like a giant Happy Meal), and one in DinoLand U.S.A. A deal with Kellogg's is also being considered.

Disney has cable channels not only in the U.S. but all over the world. Disney songs, games and characters are distributed directly to cell phones, so that subscribers can download music or even animation. A similar offering is being unveiled in the United States in 2002.

Of its theatrical productions, *Beauty and the Beast* is entering its ninth year on Broadway and to date has been produced in 14 overseas markets, and it has an international tour underway. *Lion King* is in the fifth year on Broadway and is also running in London, Toronto, Los Angeles, Hamburg, Tokyo, and Fukuoka, with a U.S. national tour in progress. *The Hunchback of Notre Dame* in in its third year in Berlin, a city record; *Aida* is set to launch a national tour company; and Disney on Ice brings in more than 8 million viewers a year. In addition, there are live-action versions of *The Little Mermaid* and *Tarzan* (perhaps using some of the roller-blading choreography of the *Tarzan Rocks!* show at Animal Kingdom) in the works.

Disney also owns three record labels: Hollywood Records,

which now primarily releases soundtracks; Mammoth, heavy on the alternative and hip-hop; and a Nashville-based country music label called Lyric Street.

Disneyland Paris (formerly known as EuroDisney), a joint venture with the French government, lost more than $900 million the first fiscal year and had to be refinanced. However, the drain slowed dramatically, and a second park is under construction there (along with hotels, a business park, a second suburban rail station, and a mixed-used "downtown" development. The Tokyo Disneyland was so successful that a second entire theme park, Tokyo DisneySea, opened in 2001. The Hong Kong park is set to open in 2005–2006.

The cruise line has just expanded its format to offer seven-day cruises with stops at Caribbean islands as well as Disney's own Castaway Cay resort, apparently to draw more grown-up passengers traveling without children.

The theme parks and resorts division continues to provide healthy increases in profits, no matter what happens to the entertainment divisions. In fact, Disney is planning to build second theme parks in both Paris and Tokyo, plus a new one in China. It's also considering launching a series of "VisionQuest" virtual reality parks.

In other words, while the headlines are trumpeting losses at ABC and theme park turnstiles, Disney's bottom line is still pretty heavy. While analysts don't expect Disney stock to recover overnight, many are predicting increasing stability and growth. (One fund purchased nearly 10 million shares shortly after September 11.) All in all, Disney executives predict that cash flow will increase as much as 20% a year.

And characteristically, Eisner intends to be front and center.

"I spend my life being Odysseus," Eisner told *Fortune* early in 2002. "I tie myself to the mast, and I don't listen to the Sirens. The Sirens in my business are agents, investment bankers, the media, people saying that your testosterone level is gone because you haven't made an acquisition in the last ten minutes.

"We've solidified our company," he continued. "When the economy turns, and when the fear of flying goes away, when we get a couple of hits on ABC—and because of how lean we've made the company—I believe it will become a gusher. I want to be here to take advantage of all the work we've done and all the crap we took. When it all comes out in the wash, we'll still be the premier growth company in our business."

Jam Yesterday, Jam Today

Walt Disney had extraordinary hopes for Epcot, the Experimental Prototype Community of Tomorrow. He envisioned it as "a showcase for American industry and research," one that would never be completely finished because it would always inspire and absorb the latest technology; a place with schools and churches but without slums ("because we won't let them develop") or landlords (nobody would own property privately); a place with office buildings but no unemployment, no welfare, and no retirement.

In building Celebration, the residential prototype at the west edge of the Disney World property, Michael Eisner has turned another Walt Disney concept around. Celebration is not the ideal community of some high-tech future, but a nice, friendly, old-fashioned American small town. The "Community of Tomorrow," built today, turns out to be . . . yesterday. And it may well be the first of Disney's most enduring contributions to early 21st-century society.

Celebration looks nothing like the retro-futuristic pyramids of Epcot. Instead of being chock-full of high-tech gadgets and monorails, it has townhouses, apartment buildings, and garages (all around the back, out of sight). Instead of laboratories and humanely designed factories, it has a school (operated by Osceola County), a complete medical center, a public golf course, and miles of biking and walking trails. Its homes are a relaxed mix of designs: Victorian, Colonial Revival, South Carolina Low Country with long front porches, Mediterranean, some with gingerbread and gables and balconies. All are old-fashioned in a nostalgic sense, nothing as modern or cool as the Swan or Dolphin hotels within the theme park. This is the architecture of the romantic-escape resorts—the Grand Floridian, the BoardWalk, Port Orleans.

In fact, along its downtown boulevards, Market Street and Front Street, there are four restaurants, shops, a bank, a market, a town hall, and a small two-screen cinema—just the sorts of businesses Walt Disney chose for his past-perfect Main Street,

U.S.A. Only this time, the apartments over the businesses are real. If Michael Eisner has limited the technological flash of Walt Disney's vision, he has held on to its heart. (It also has a hotel, for those who want to visit this ultimate "attraction.")

Celebration's most Eisner-era elements are its name-brand architects—a dozen firms, including Phillip Johnson's and Michael Graves', contributed either to the town's overall planning or to its actual buildings—and its cost. Originally proposed as a middle-income town, it's a little more upscale than that, with houses ranging from $160,000 to $1 million. (Apartments rent for about $850 to $2,500 a month.) Even at that price, there was so much interest that prospective residents had to put down refundable deposits in order to be in a lottery to become one of the first 500 buyers or renters. It is already home to the 20,000 residents Walt envisioned for Epcot—most of whom are not, contrary to some rumors, Disney cast members—and it is being expanded.

Clearly, it is Walt's America that glimmers in Celebration. In a *New Yorker* article by architecture critic Witold Rybczynski, project planner Tom Lewis says Celebration "could have been a second-home community or a resort or a retirement village. Instead, we decided that it would be a place where families would have their primary residences. We wanted it to be a real town"—like Pinocchio, the puppet who had to learn to listen to his heart to become a real boy.

And it was developer James Rouse who in 1963 told the graduating class of Harvard architecture school that Disneyland was "the outstanding piece of urban design in the United States [in its] performance, in its respect for people, in its functioning for people." It was also Rouse, with his own back-to–Main Street new town of Columbia, Maryland, and waterfront revitalization projects in Boston's Faneuil Hall and Baltimore's Harborplace, who pushed for the return of planned communities like Celebration.

Creationism

Backstage and Below Ground

In its seamless melding of function and fantasy, Walt Disney World is a marvel. Elements had to be reconsidered and then re-created; materials had to be perfectly imitated and often improved (fireproofed, strengthened, infinitely replicated); gears and gadgets had to be imagined, engineered, and then—poof!—made invisible. All this became the responsibility of the Imagineers.

In the term "Imagineer" (a contraction of "imagine" and "engineer"), the imagination part comes first, and that's how Walt Disney intended it to work. The Imagineers were assigned to plan, design, engineer, and supervise the whole theme park as they had Disneyland. This is more peculiar than it sounds. The original Imagineers were artists and animators, not builders. They wouldn't have been able to design a building the traditional way even if Walt had wanted them to, which he didn't. To guarantee that they were insulated from any pushy company directors or budget crunchers, Walt created a private company and paid the Imagineers out of his own private pocket. The company was originally called WED Enterprises, in his honor. It was brought into the Disney Company in 1964, by which time it was a safely successful and much admired team of writers, computer geeks, researchers, industrial designers, architects, audio and film techies, and so on. (Though the Imagineering section remains fairly independent, just recently President Michael Eisner reshuffled the corporation to put that operation in with theme parks and attractions.)

Whereas most real-world architecture is at least conceived with the utilities, light, and traffic flow worked right in, the attractions at Disney World are "drawn" like cartoons, like the preliminary sketches for an animated film; then the pulleys and levers have to be made to fit the picture. So virtually everything about the parks, from the physical structures to the rides to the special effects, was invented as if the rules of practical construction had been suspended. In fact, they had.

Even today the Imagineers plot rides on storyboards first, getting the "look" not only from the designer's viewpoint but from the passenger's as well. After that, a scale model is built and juggled around before blueprints are drawn and the actual logistics are figured out. (Curiosity-seekers should keep their eyes open as they ride through Space Mountain on the Tomorrowland Transit Authority for the model representing the original concept for Epcot, only about 10 by 20 feet.) When the design for an attraction is fairly set, it's passed over to what was for many years called MAPO, an acronym of "Mary Poppins," whose strange combination of magic and no-nonsense neatness is the perfect model for the development and manufacturing arm of the company (and whose incredible movie success provided the seed money for Walt Disney World itself). Nowadays, sadly, the division goes by the more prosaic title of "Manufacturing and Production Organization," even though the various Disney-trivia–game computers installed for the "100 Years of Magic" celebration still have a question about the acronym's origin.

But that doesn't mean the Imagineers don't do in-depth research. In fact, before designing the Asia section of Animal Kingdom, Imagineers visited Nepal (to go river rafting), Thailand (to go elephant trekking), Bhutan, Bali, Java, and Singapore, and had their skins henna-tattooed in India.

Perhaps the best example of classical Imagineering, inside and out, is Cinderella Castle. First came the "look": Cinderella Castle sums up the Imagineers' bigger-and-better-than-life architectural style (the castle has 10 spires, a Romanesque base, Gothic arches, and Renaissance rococo Bavarian turrets); their pragmatism (the "stone blocks" are made of fiberglass over steel); their obsessive craftsmanship (the five 15-foot mosaic panels in the foyer took a million chips and two years to complete); their whimsy (the "Disney crest" is carved over the great entrance); and their sheer, almost childlike brilliance (the entire five-ton pinnacle of the tower unscrews in case of hurricanes).

Then came the "background." Where the castle now stands, where almost the entire Magic Kingdom now stands, was the rawest swamp—12 feet "deeper" than the park is now—until dredging produced an island and a square mile of Seven Seas Lagoon. Then the wheels and pulleys went in: a suite of apartments originally designed for the Disney family (but never inhabited), a security station in the central tower, and a broadcast center that monitors the progress of the various parades. The second floor houses the restaurant, Cinderella's Royal Table. There are three elevators in the Castle, as well as intricate water and ventilation equipment. And, although there are no bats in the Castle belfry, there are pigeons in the palace: One of the top turrets is the "dove cote" (really the loft where the white homing pigeons roost between parades).

But the real magic is down at dungeon level. What seem to be the foundation of the Castle and the Royal Table are actually its second and third stories. Underneath, in the reclaimed swamp, is the Utilidor (contraction of "utility corridor"), a mile of tunnels spoking out in all directions through the Magic Kingdom. At one brilliant stroke, the Utilidor solved three problems: It reduced the amount of fill dirt needed under the park; it allowed all nonmagical elements—wiring, garbage, computer operators, and even characters out of costume—to be hidden from sight; and it cut travel time for employees and maintenance staff to scant minutes, because they didn't have to negotiate crowds or public routes.

The Utilidor was constructed above ground, to avoid water seeping in. It probably started out looking like a parking garage. The tunnels, as high as 15 feet, are wide enough to allow tractor-trains of supply carts to pass; the utility lines are marked and within reach; and there are honeycombs of studios and storerooms all around. The hot and cold water pipes, the air conditioning vents and smoke-removal fans, and even the fiber-optic lines and computer hookups are all here in the Utilidor. Pneumatic tubes (the sort that used to carry copy from newsrooms to typesetters in the old days) automatically transfer waste from the surface to garbage trucks in the basement. So guests never see more than a small can of trash, and certainly never any of the dump trucks, which emerge at the ends of the tunnels some distance away. The various tunnels were painted different colors as code for the different theme areas, so that cast members couldn't get lost and show up in the wrong place; theme park pictures were later added for the benefit of color-blind cast members.

The whole thing was then roofed and covered over with eight million cubic yards of dirt dredged from Seven Seas Lagoon, hiding the Utilidor "underground," and the Castle was built on top. The Magic Kingdom, in other words, is several yards above original ground level—a castle in the air.

This underground complex is now the home of many of the DACs and AMCs—Digital Animation Control and Automatic Monitor Control systems—that monitor and control many of the park's environmental systems, including energy consumption, refrigeration, resort and restaurant reservations, and even the Muzak. The computers lie under The Haunted Mansion, in one of the most closely guarded areas.

The Utilidor is also one of the major "cast" areas of the theme park. As many as 8,000 employees are there in a day, among them the video and film technicians, tailors, wigmakers and makeup artists, maintenance workers, animators, and computer operators. (Here's an amazing figure: The Magic Kingdom alone produces 68 tons of dirty laundry and 115 pounds of dryer lint every single day.)

The Utilidor was a deep secret for many years, but these days interested guests can see parts of it by taking either of the behind-the-scenes tours called Keys to the Kingdom or Backstage Magic. Epcot has a much smaller version of a Utilidor, because the pavilions, which in effect constitute the outer perimeter of the World Showcase, can be serviced from the back without the guests' knowledge. However, the computer center for that theme park is also below ground, 20 feet under Innoventions East.

Right Before Your Very Eyes . . .

Imagineering calls for a good eye—and also for knowing how to fool one. When he was designing Disneyland, Walt had been more focused on eliciting a sense of nostalgia and security, so he built everything to a kind of playhouse scale, five-eighths of its real size. But when it came to Disney World, Walt Disney wanted his ideal Main Street to be a vital, comfortable area for shopping and eating. The stores and restaurants had to be at least close to real size, even if they were crowded. So the Imagineers, drawing on their drawings, used the old artist's trick of artificial perspective: they made the upper stories a little smaller so that they *looked* as if they were stretching even higher into the sky. Therefore, the ground floors are 90% life size, the second floors, 80%, and any third-floor attics even smaller, only 60% real size. This also makes the street seem longer than it actually is: only three football fields from the railroad station to the Castle wall. (Even the speed of the "average guest" was figured into the design—three miles an hour.) But none of the space is wasted; the apparent second-floor rooms are only about three feet deep, and behind the false walls are offices and storage with other, real windows facing out the back.

Imagineers also have ways of fooling the ear and the nose. In certain rides, as particular cars pass, the "background noises" grow louder in order to help pull the observer into the picture. In the rain forest region of The Land, the animals and birds are cued by sensors to seem alarmed by the human's presence. Sometimes it's just a matter of the details, as with the horseless carriages of Main Street, which have Jeep transmissions but specially designed mufflers that go *putta-dutta-dut* as if the two cylinders inside were struggling along.

The susceptibility of the human nose is so great that the right scent can sometimes produce three-dimensional hallucinations. Disney's air fresheners are so powerful that they're nicknamed "smellitzers," a name play on howitzer cannons. Sulphur is "fired" into the air at Ellen's Energy Adventure, where volcanoes are spewing and dinosaurs are putrefying into fuel oil. Some more cheerful aromas provide atmosphere and encourage consumption at the same time, like the air blown from around the chocolate chip cookie shop into Main Street. And some, like the dual-scented curtain of mist along the Kali River Rapids ride, serve as a subconscious premonition, like violins on a soundtrack: in this case, the mist is perfumed with jasmine as you enter but smells of burning forest as you emerge toward the illegal logging site.

Lighting effects have always been a part of Walt Disney World—there are several fireworks and special-effects light shows in the park every evening—but they get more high-tech every year. The Magic Kingdom's SpectroMagic parade involves giant prismatic holographs, military lighting, light-spreading thermoplastics, liquid nitrogen "smoke" (a sinuous improvement on the traditional dry ice), and electroluminescent and fiber-optic technology, in addition to the traditional fluorescent bulbs—a mere 600,000 of them—and mirrors. The audio is stored digitally on microchips and triggered sequentially by sensors along the route.

The Floating Electrical Pageant is SpectroMagic on the half shell: a barge parade starring King Neptune (who does, after all, make an appearance in SpectroMagic, along with his daughter Ariel) and cruising around Bay Lake to Handel's "Royal Fireworks Music." *IllumiNations*, the after-dark show at Epcot's World Showcase Lagoon, involves a mixture of laser lights and fireworks. Disney-MGM Studios has *Fantasmic!*, a mixed laser, fireworks, and "dancing waters" display based on Mickey's famous exploits as the Sorcerer's Apprentice in *Fantasia*. It fills its own amphitheater behind the Tower of Terror, over its own lagoon.

High Ho, Heigh-Ho, It's Off to Work We Go . . .

Two of the three tallest mountains in Florida are at Disney World, and neither of them owes anything to nature. Big Thunder Mountain is 197 feet tall, and Space Mountain is 180 feet. How they got there is a story in itself.

Walt Disney World's Big Thunder Mountain has the film-industry pedigree one might expect: It's modeled after Monument Valley, the area director John Ford used in such classic western films as *Stagecoach*. According to the "official" Birnbaum guide to Walt Disney World, it took 15 years to plan and almost two years to build, requiring layering 4,500 tons of cement over 650 tons of steel and covering that with 5,000 tons of artificial mud and 16,000 gallons of paint. The whole thing weighs 65 tons. After that, the Imagineers called in the strike force to beat the surface with picks, throw stones at it, and toss clods of earth on it to give it that "weathered" look. The result is so realistic that cast members report having to dissuade rattled rattlesnakes from trying to find homes there.

Big Thunder Mountain also exhibits a great example of the Imagineers' less-expensive ingenuity: The apparently well-aged and "bubbled" exterior of the saloon is the result of mixing plant food into the paint.

Space Mountain, whose shape is a gentle homage to Japan's serene Mount Fuji, is obviously artificial, but its design—72 pre-stressed concrete beams 117 feet long, and gradually decreasing from 13 feet across at the bottom to 4 feet at the top—is equally impressive in a technical way. And Space Mountain's cheap trick? Chocolate chip cookies, magnified and slightly nibbled, that moonlight as meteorites.

The "high points" all over Walt Disney World have an invisible ceiling, since Florida law requires a flashing beacon on any structure 200 feet tall or higher. Spaceship Earth is 180 feet tall, Cinderella Castle tops out at 189 feet, Big Thunder Mountain peaks at 197 feet, and *The Twilight Zone* Tower of Terror is 199 feet tall—after all, a bravely flashing light on top of the Tower might cramp its dark and scary style.

Even leaving out the cookies, the sheer number and variety of materials used in Walt Disney World is astonishing. There are more than 20,000 paint colors, along with the items on which they are used, catalogued in the main computer. The mosaics in Cinderella Castle have more than 500 shades of glass, as well as sterling silver and 14-karat gold. And sometimes re-creating a period effect means relearning period techniques. All the costumes for the Audio-Animatronic presidents for instance—and each has a spare outfit—were handmade using appropriate sewing methods of the times.

One of the most famous "trees" in Disney World is the one that supports the Swiss Family Treehouse, a classic example of the Imagineers' art. The tree, labeled *Disneyodendron eximus,* or "extraordinary Disney tree," by corporate wags, is 90 feet across, stands 90 feet above the ground, and reaches nearly half as far below. It weighs more than 200 tons, thanks to its steel structure, stucco bark, and concrete roots. It has 1,400 branches, and it is altogether so amazing a feat, and such an obvious symbol of Disney's determination to better nature, that Professor Fjellman named his book *Vinyl Leaves* in honor of its 300,000 plastic attachments.

But the tree created for the Animal Kingdom quite literally dwarfs its older brother, standing 145 feet tall, the equivalent of a 14-story building, with a trunk 50 feet wide and roots and branches up to 170 feet across (there are 8,000 of those branches, and they're flexible enough to bend in the wind). Its frame is a modified oil derrick, which was necessary to support the concrete of the trunk and limbs; and though not brushing the park's invisible ceiling, it's visible from points all around Walt Disney World, including the peak of Blizzard Beach and the California Grill on top of the Contemporary Resort.

It took two years to "grow" to this size: The original foundation was poured in fall 1995, and a team of sculptors worked six days a week for two years to complete the mazelike exterior. The exterior—which resembles one of those children's puzzles in which the mane of the lion fits into the feathers of the cockatoo, whose beak meets the alligator's teeth, and so on—includes some 350 figures, including some that are in the "roots" visible as you circle down to the *It's Tough to Be a Bug!* show inside.

Inside is an entire theater that seats 425 and has special effects seats, not unlike those at *Honey, I Shrunk the Audience* (not to give anything away), as well as visual effects from both the Imagineers and Pixar, the computer animation company founded by former Apple Computers president Steve Jobs. Pixar also coproduced *It's a Bug's Life* and *Toy Story.*

Some Imagineered effects are necessary concessions to modern life: The Percherons and Belgian draft horses that pull the trolleys along Main Street wear shoes that are steel covered with polyurethane, but the blacksmith at Fort Wilderness works on them the old-fashioned way with anvil and forge. The Mark VII race cars at the Tomorrowland Speedway only hit seven miles per hour in their little track runs, but they do burn real gasoline and cost a respectable $6,000 apiece.

Some environments are real but anomalous, plucked out of their natural settings and brought to Walt Disney World for effect. Even Discovery Island, that little island that captured Walt's heart, had to be entirely re-created by being cleared of scrub, spread with 15,000 cubic yards of soil that was then pushed up into hills and down into pools, topped with 1,000 tons of trees and rocks, and finally planted with hundreds of species of plants and trees from South and Central America, Japan, India, and China. Sadly, these plants may have to be scrubbed themselves if the island is to be returned to preserve status.

Sometimes the Imagineers seem to be singing, "Anything you can do, I can do better." Does Old Faithful spout every 6½ minutes? The Fire Rock geyser at Wilderness Lodge will erupt every hour on the hour except between 10 p.m. and 8 a.m., when somebody might be sleeping.

And sometimes it just seems as though they couldn't refuse a dare. As famous as Buckminster Fuller's geodesic domes were, almost none were ever built. Spaceship Earth is actually two of them—two domes put together into a *geosphere* that spans 165 feet in diameter and 180 feet in height, with an outer shell made of 954 aluminum triangles and a sort of inner tube, 20 feet smaller, of steel and waterproof lining. The globe weighs 8,000 tons, and—a really weird piece of trivia—it's been calculated that if the Spaceship were a golf ball, the matching driver would be close to a mile high.

Most Imagineering is a strange combination of real and surreal, or Ur-real. The original 72 horses on Cinderella's Golden Carrousel were hand-carved 80 years ago in elaborate detail by Italian employees of the Philadelphia Toboggan Company. But by the time Disney scouts found them in Olympic Park in Maplewood, New Jersey, in the mid-1960s, layers of paint had obscured the fine work. The horses were stripped and repainted (all as white as a princess's steed, but each with an individually painted harness), their legs repositioned, and 18 more carved in exact imitation.

At Madame Lafayette's Parfumerie in Liberty Square, fragrances are custom-mixed to the patron's liking, but any one can be reordered because its "unique" formula is computerized. The birds and animals of the Jungle Cruise are all Audio-Animatronic, but the sounds were carefully recorded in Africa and South America for authenticity.

The plants in Living with the Land are all plastic; the tree trunks and branches were meticulously molded from living trees; and the blades of grass a fire-retardant blend of glass and rubber, but the "rain," which precipitates out of the air from the artificially maintained humidity, is in at least some sense real. In the greenhouses where the experimental and hydroponic gardening techniques are displayed, the plants and the water are real but the soil is artificial. The Swiss Family Treehouse tree is man-made, but the Spanish moss hanging on it is real.

The buffalo rifles in the Frontierland Shootin' Gallery are genuine Hawkins 54-calibers, but they have been modified to shoot infrared beams. Some of Main Street's wooden planks are really fiberglass, but the wooden pegs are real. Much of the antique mining equipment on Big Thunder Mountain is real, and the "rust" on the rest is half-real: it's ground-up rust bonded in resin to the top of rust-proof steel bolts. The whitewash on the fence at Tom Sawyer Island looks real enough, but it's actually liquid chalk. Because of this, as many kids as want to can paint every day, and maintenance staff can hose the fence clean every night. The totem poles outside Wilderness Lodge are authentic Pacific carvings, but the "hot spring" that feeds the swimming pool and the geyser are artificial. The colonial-style shell of *The American Adventure* isn't colonial and the Audio-Animatronic Americans aren't real, of course—but the 110,000 bricks are, made by hand from Georgia clay.

The lake that formerly held the 20,000 Leagues Under the Sea ride is a typical conglomerate of natural and artificial elements. The shell, which holds 11½ million gallons of water, is steel and fiberglass; the rocks are steel covered with plastic; and the starfish, barnacles, and mollusks are all cast-fiberglass copies. River Country's rocks are a mix of plaster-covered steel, fiberglass, cement, and real rocks "imported" from Georgia and the Carolinas (the same rocks used in the Japan Pavilion in Epcot).

Speaking of that Japan pavilion, the pagoda's five stories represent earth, wind, fire, water, and sky; the trees are real, but the wood of the harbor gate and even the iron hitching ring are not. And if you look closely, you will see that even the "straw thatch" of the roof on the cottage at the United Kingdom complex is synthetic. The benches at Animal World are made from recycled milk jugs (about 3,500 jugs per seat).

Even more elaborate a construction is Epcot's "Caribbean coral reef" in The Living Seas. It's a 28-foot-deep concrete tank, with a "reef" made of fiberglass and silicone. It is filled with over 5½ million gallons of imitation sea water that has to be constantly recycled and filtered to maintain its various salts and minerals in a sort of reverse version of a swimming pool pump. Here at least the starfish and such are real, but the coral is not. Nor is it real in the Pacific coral lagoon tank or any of the other pools in the pavilion, and some of the coral-dwelling fish have to be diverted from eating it. The living fish, hundreds of varieties of them, eat frozen fish, hundreds of pounds of them.

The Animal Kingdom's 110-acre Serengeti-inspired savannah is also part real, part set. Because so many of the animals actually eat the "landscape," Disney maintains an eight-acre "browsing farm" to grow mulberries, shrubs, hibiscus, and vegetables. Aside from the Tree of Life, the major artificial trees in the Animal Kingdom are concrete baobabs that are secretly hung with rotating leaves intended to tempt the giraffes (although rumors have it they aren't crazy about this buffet service).

The "mud tracks" on the safari ride are molded cement, sprinkled with twigs, pebbles, and dirt. The safari vehicles are converted GMC trucks running on propane. Some of the rocks on which the big cats loll are actually climate-controlled concrete bunkers. The Imagineers hoped this would encourage the lions and tigers to be visible more often, but this, too, has had only partial success.

Some of the finest imitations were created to bolster the illusion that there are no barriers between the animals and the humans: The "bamboo" that separates the gorilla family on the Pagnani trail are actually steel bars, and though there seems to be only a grassy marsh between, the chasm is quite deep. On the other hand, the bamboo scaffolding around the temple in the Asia section is real.

And then, of course, there's DinoLand U.S.A., where most of the skeletons are reproductions (not real fossils but cast from them), but also where the actual skeleton of "Sue," the 65-million-year-old *Tyrannosaurus rex,* is in fact being exposed and preserved for the Field Museum of Natural History in Chicago.

This mix of simulation and authenticity becomes an in-joke in a park built on the movie industry, such as Disney-MGM Studios. Building facades, perspective effects, and false backgrounds are the reality of film. While Epcot offers half-sized but faithful replicas of such landmarks as the Gate of Heaven in Beijing, a Mayan temple in Mexico, or the Doge's Palace in Venice, Disney-MGM offers a full-scale version of Mann's Chinese Theatre, but only a couple of feet thick. At the Magic Kingdom, the subtle forced perspective of building looks real to the eye; at Disney-MGM, the backdrops of New York City are painted in visibly forced perspective that is obvious to the eye.

And because Disney-MGM Studios is all about movie-making, the puns get double-layered. For instance, at the *Indiana Jones Stunt Spectacular,* all the apparent crew members, the prop people, the sound techies, etc., are part of the show, just actors. The real sound people are out of sight—and even they aren't really "sound people" any more either, but computer techies in charge of fully automatic disks and electronic cueing.

Catastrophe Canyon, a set-up version of a special effects scene of an earthquake and fire, seems like a mirror version of Big Thunder Mountain until passengers are shown the gas pipes that supply the "fire." (But it's highly unlikely that in this litigious age—and in this incredibly expensive setup—that the real gas pipes are exposed to potential tampering or damage.) The supposedly real-life experiments in sound editing, blue-screen formatting, and model shooting that are part of the MGM Studios Tour are only semi-real, temporary overlays that are never really mixed into the digital production. The animators in the studio are obviously real, but the Oscars in the lobby are just reproductions.

The see-through robot at *Alien Encounter,* who looks like a combination of C-3PO and the old "Visible Body" models, is a real Audio-Animatronic figure but a fake robot, since at least some of the wiring is cosmetic.

Now that virtual reality has entered the picture, the combination of "real" and "unreal" is even more complicated. At Eclectronics in the Innoventions pavilion at Epcot, you can take a virtual-reality tour guided by an Audio-Animatronic host; or check out the Walt Disney Imagineering Laboratory and their virtual-reality plans for the fantasy ride based on the animated *Aladdin.* That's a virtual-reality visit with a virtual being—or virtually real virtual-reality visions of a virtually real theme park.

"I Want to Be a Real Boy"

Walt Disney's long effort to develop lifelike robots goes back to the 1930s, when he tinkered with hydraulically manipulated giant dolls that sat on top of their machinery like huge, clumsy jacks-in-the-box. His obsession also suggests a certain bittersweet element to one of his best-loved cartoons: *Pinocchio,* the story of a marionette (and his aging, avuncular creator) who becomes more and more human until he finally becomes a real boy.

From the early animal robots that had only one or two movements (the Tiki Room birds, hippos that opened their mouths and sank back, etc.), to the elaborate C-3PO-like host at *Alien Encounter* and his Robin Williams parody over at *The Timekeeper,* Disney's Audio-Animatronics have become more and more impressive. The Alien itself is no slouch, as a matter of fact, and the Audio-Animatronic dinosaurs at Animal Kingdom are breathtaking. And the attention to detail is, as always, stunning: There are 10 different species of dinosaurs, each readily identifiable to knowledgeable observers, in the Universe of Energy alone.

The Audio-Animatronics are first modeled on a small scale in clay, and then a second full-size model is made. Next comes a hollow plastic body (a sort of test run for the high-tech innards), followed by a plastic body molded from the clay to make a "skin" of a vinyl synthetic called Duraflex that, as its name suggests, stretches and flexes. The compressed-air hoses and valves that move the body are the same as those used in space suits. Tiny electric relays are installed around the corners of the mouths and eyes to increase the realism of facial expressions. Then, just as live actors and actresses are filmed acting out cartoon scripts so that their animated versions can be drawn as exactly as possible, real people are studied and turned into computer film so that the Audio-Animatronics' movements can be programmed in as a flood of electronic bytes. In a way, it's another virtual-reality game, except that the perceived video is "memorized" by the robot.

The hair is human, the costumes hand- or machine-stitched, depending on the time period returned to; even the button material is reputed to be authentic to the era.

Although they can be slow and stiff, the Audio-Animatronics fascinate their audiences. One man entering *The Hall of Presidents* for what was clearly the third or fourth time, insisted, "I want to get down close enough to see their lips move—I've always been too far back."

It isn't just their lips that have to move, or that require astonishing leaps of technology to do so. In *The American Adventure,* during which the robot figures enter, exit, row, write, and ride horseback, the characters—including three or four separate Ben Franklins and Mark Twains, each with different speeches—are grouped along a vast moveable underground stage. Nicknamed the "war wagon," it rolls back and forth from side to side in order to hoist the sets and Audio-Animatronic speakers into place. (Ben doesn't really walk up the stairs: he's gently boosted up one step at a time.) The wagon weighs 175 tons, so great a weight that the surface beneath it has 300-foot-deep pilings. If you sit close enough, you can hear the gears turning and the poor thing creaking. But then, that's what earthquakes are, too—the sets moving around.

Bigger, Better, Faster, Scarier

There is a moment during the *Alien Encounter* ride in which the megalomaniacal multibillionaire from another galaxy, president of XS Tech, says with irresistible flourish, "If something can't be done with XS, it shouldn't be done at all." It sounds like an in-house joke: After the first time Disney CEO Michael Eisner sat through the $60 million ride that, theatrically speaking, lets the Alien loose to snack on the strapped-in passengers, Eisner sent it back to the Imagineers' drawing board because it wasn't scary enough. (The improvements included the hot breath on the back of passengers' necks, the "blood" that sprays the room, and the night vision film.) *The Twilight Zone* Tower of Terror recently got a 100% boost in scariness, so to speak—a third jolt, and then a fourth, just when you thought it was safe to let your breath out.

That doesn't happen very often, because Disney Imagineers are usually on the leading edge of special effects. Body Wars in Epcot, Star Tours in Disney-MGM Studios, and the Dinosaur ride in Animal Kingdom all use flight simulators, adapted from aircraft simulation training installations, to produce the sensations of take-off, rapid transit, landing, turbulence, or even free fall and collision. Each simulator can be adapted into a 40-seat theater and perform 26 movements that, synchronized with the films, "persuade" the inner ear of acceleration and imbalance, although the actual give is only a few feet in any direction. Star Tours and Body Wars each use four of these simulators, at a cost of a half-million dollars apiece. And since the video and synchronized effects of the simulators—the script—can be updated without much structural work, the next generation of rides will almost certainly involve computer-generated virtual-reality technology.

Disney is already using virtual reality to remarkable effect—not only keeping up with the art, but often pushing it forward. The 1990s 3-D effects of *Captain EO* were a revelation to many, but the VR punch of *Honey, I Shrunk the Audience, MuppetVision 4D,* and *It's Tough to Be a Bug!* is a leap beyond that. Instead of the old red-green glasses, the new technology involves a sort of two-eyed camera, one whose simultaneously filming lenses are about two inches apart, like human eyes, and the film is a special high-speed format with polarized film interspersed every several frames. Unlike *EO,* in which the effects were truest in the center, the audience technology makes the holographic images convincing from any place in the room. Combined with smoke, fiber-optics, water "sliming," and moveable seats—not to mention little feathery "mouse tails" underneath the chairs—it's pretty amazing. In fact, we defy anyone to resist flinching from the breaking glass.

Apparent movement doesn't require much real space. The "descent" into The Living Seas' "Sea Base Alpha," which seems to be about 50 feet and takes 30 seconds, actually is only a couple of inches. It is made to feel deeper by vibrations, lighting changes, bubbles that suggest pressure changes, and scenery that rises—fooling the mind just the way a car rolling forward next to you can make you feel as if you're rolling backward. In the *Carousel of Progress,* the "ride," in this case the stage, doesn't move at all: The audience rotates around it. And some of the super–wide screen films, like the Circle-Vision 360° film segment of *The Timekeeper,* were shot at such speed (in this case, up to 60 miles per hour along the bobsled run) that your stomach may also shoot the hairpin curve.

Imagineers are so accustomed to pushing the special effects envelope that they have been working for some time on a "weightlessness" chamber for the Mission: Space attraction at Epcot. And with Disney's usual emphasis on authenticity, it has hired six-time shuttle astronaut Story Musgrave as a consultant on the project, which is intended to reproduce the experience of space travel. However, the technology has so far frustrated even these masters of magic, though no one is as yet counting them out—just wondering whether the 2003 opening date will be pushed back (with the park-wide post-9/11 slowdown, it may not even be obvious).

When it comes to creating scary rides with unsimulated movement, however, speed is of the essence, because it exaggerates the degree to which the rider feels off balance, cut loose, or out of control. The cars in Space Mountain and Big Thunder Mountain hit about 28 miles per hour; Splash Mountain reportedly works up to a top speed of 40, with a 52-foot drop at a 45° angle. The monorail trains are theoretically capable of doing close to 100 miles per hour, but they generally cruise at about 40. But none of those comes close to the stomach punch provided by the repeated "13-story" deadfall drops in *The Twilight Zone* Tower of Terror, which some people have guessed hit 45 miles per hour.

The race is on all over the World. The Rock 'n' Roller Coaster off Sunset Boulevard at Disney-MGM Studios winds through the fretboard of a huge guitar, the hole in the center of a 45-rpm record (if anyone remembers those), and through one of the "O"s in a replica of the "HOLLYWOOD" sign built on the hillside overlooking the studios. Appropriately enough, the ride also hits 45 miles per hour. But at least there, passengers ride in pink big-fin Cadillacs. "Skiers" running the 120-foot Summit Plummet drop at Blizzard Beach are said to hit 60 miles per hour in only their bathing suits.

The Test Track ride, which is the centerpiece of the renovated World of Motion Pavilion at Epcot takes passengers through a one-mile simulation of the all-terrain, all-weather testing to which manufacturers subject new cars at 45 miles per hour. There is an outside section of curved track (visible from the backstage parking lot if you take certain behind-the-scenes tours) and a crash test in which you may bust through the "wall" of the building. Got your seatbelt on?

The Fun Factory

"Whistle While You Work"

"Imagineering" Walt Disney World is a mammoth and perpetual undertaking, but nobody ever said it wasn't fun. The Disney creative engineering team was dosed with the original pixie dust— Walt's personal affection and trust—and their dedication to his vision includes building in the whimsy, the warmth, and the sly film and cultural references that provided visual puns in even Disney's earliest cartoons. Animation was never kid stuff, not really, and aside from the specific design challenges, the Imagineers were determined to build just those sorts of little puns and pleasures into the park. Besides, it was more fun for them.

Many of the original Imagineers, as well as some of the executives, have hidden "credits" around the park. The joke tombstones at The Haunted Mansion refer to art directors, Imagineers, and scriptwriters; the five singing busts in the graveyard, the heads in the library, and the fortune teller in the crystal ball represent animators, voice-over artists (including Paul "Boris" Badenov and Thurl "Tony the Tiger" Ravenscroft), wardrobe designers, and illusionists. Faces in the crowds and murals in *The American Adventure* and *The Hall of Presidents* are based on artists and Imagineers.

Names on crates at the Jungle Cruise and on shops along Main Street are also tributes, especially to those who were present at the creation, so to speak: Dick Nunis, chief of operations during the building of the park and then president, is said to run the gym. "I Associates," as in Imagineers, bears the name of one-time Walt Disney Productions president Card Walker as resident shrink. The names "Bill Davis," one of Disney's pseudonyms, and Bob Foster, one of the real estate attorneys who managed the great Orlando purchase, are on the sign of the hilariously frank "Pseudonym Real Estate Development Co." There's also an M. T. Lott Real Estate Investments firm. Richard Irvine, and Admiral Joe Fowler and General Joe Potter—the two engineering veterans who helped give the construction plans for Disney World some much-needed plausibility—are saluted by the eponymous water shuttles to the Magic Kingdom. Ub Iwerks got a visual, as well as audial pun (say EyeWorks) in the sign for "Iwerks-Iwerks Stereoscopes."

Walt's name is on the second floor of the ice cream parlor, facing the Castle; brother Roy is listed as offering sailing lessons. Imagineer Roger E. Broggie has a train named after him, as do Walt, his wife Lillian (a.k.a. "Lilly Belle"), and Roy Disney. In the mosaics beneath Cinderella Castle, the page placing Cinderella's slipper on her foot is a somewhat caricatured Disney artist Herb Ryman, and the other page watching is Imagineer John Hench. A note on the wall at the *Carousel of Progress* says, "Marty called—wants changes!", a reference to Chief of Imagineering Marty Sklar. In Spaceship Earth, among the pictures of the teenagers' movie idols of the 1940s is a photo of Walt Disney. In the rafters of DinoLand U.S.A.'s Boneyard Playground, there are shoes marked "DKG 6-5-70" and "RHW 6-16-70," almost certainly the "tracks" of Imagineers.

For all its very up-to-date corporate outlook, the Disney Company has made at least one totally sentimental move in honor of Walt Disney World's first quarter-century: the long-time park logo, in which the capital "D" was squared off to enclose the globe with the Mickey Mouse ears, has been quietly replaced by Walt Disney's own signature, with the word "World" added on. Calculated to advertise the company's old-fashioned family values? Maybe—but you gotta like it anyway.

He's Everywhere! He's Everywhere!

Walt Disney never stopped reminding his employees that they owed their kingdom to a mouse, but if Mickey cast a long shadow over the company, it was a beloved one. One of the most endearing hobbies the Imagineers have is hiding Mickey heads in every nook and cranny—Mickey "logos," made up of one large circle and two smaller ones at 10 and 2 o'clock; Mickey "ears" like Mouseketeer hats (half-circles with smaller circles above); heads with pointed hats, from the Sorcerer's Apprentice segment of *Fantasia;* and Mickey silhouettes, with little raisin noses (and both ears, since Mickey's auditory appendages somehow pivot so as to be roundly visible from every angle). If you've seen the television commercials for the Disney Cruise Line in which shadows of humans have ears, fireworks round off, and so on, you have an idea what these now-you-see-'em, now-you-don't Mickeys are like.

These are not the intentional or "blatant" Mickeys such as the water tower at MGM Studios, known as the Earful Tower (which, interestingly, was not constructed to hold water), or Mickey topiaries; nor are they "decor" Mickeys printed on plates or programs, or cooked into waffles or pizzas (or pizza menus—check out that pepperoni picture!), or molded in butter. These are shapes you could (and probably will) pass right by at least once in the blur of park life. They are overhead, underfoot, in sets, in shops, in shadows, in shrubs—even, if you stay in some of the hotels, in the patterned wrapping of rolls of toilet paper. (The power line "pole" at Downtown Disney is anything by treelike.) They are tiny, huge, drawn, three-dimensional, in films, and in facades. They're in the theme parks, the resort hotels, the restaurants, and even in some of the recreational areas. According to cast legend, there is at least one Hidden Mickey in every ride and amusement in the entire World; they just haven't all been found yet.

They range from the fairly obvious floral plantings, like the plot in the middle of the Main Street entrance; to the slightly more subtle, like the three-lobed cactus target in the Frontierland Shootin' Gallery; to the most elaborately constructed shadows, like the one that fleetingly appears as a Lost Boy swoops by in Peter Pan's Flight. If you count the Mickeys in various fence railings, bas-relief patterns, café transoms, and so on, there are thousands. Count the carpets, the shopping bags—look at the shape of the "stars" around the drawing of Cinderella Castle—those laundry supplies, and who knows how many exist.

In fact, if you look at Disney's online sites carefully, you can find shopping items, D-cards, hotel room plans, and even hyperlinks that are Mickey-shaped. And some people believe that the lightning-bolt logo for the Disney-owned Touchstone Pictures is a very stretched-out Mickey profile.

Nobody does know, in fact, exactly how many Hidden Mickeys there are. Some are reported on Disney-freak World Wide Web sites and then "flamed" as wishful thinking; some are erased by renovations; some are on such deep background only certain cast members are ever in a position to see them. (Any time you're waiting in line, ask the nearest cast member to show you one. Chances are at least one is within sight.)

There is, however, at least one respectful exception; there are no hidden Mickeys in *The Hall of Presidents*. And no one's spotted any in Typhoon Lagoon yet, either.

Finding Hidden Mickeys is a full-time hobby with some fans. The Disney Channel's *Walt Disney World Inside Out* program has finally acknowledged the fascination visitors have with the puzzles, and a couple of websites are devoted to listing only those "vanished" Mickeys that have been renovated out of existence (not to mention the several pages devoted to recording new ones). The following are some examples that show both the humor and the fondness the Imagineers have for their mascot.

Some are built into ride "sets": In the *Carousel of Progress,* the mother's computer screen flashes a Mickey screen saver, and there are Mickeys and Disney references all over the Christmas scene, from the wrapping paper to the nutcracker to the salt and pepper shakers. (At press time, CoP, as it's known to fans, was "seasonally closed," but staff rumor suggested the veteran attraction might not be reopened.) In the Tomorrowland Transit Authority, in the "Take Flight" scene where a woman is having her hair done, there is a Mickey head on her belt buckle. He's also in the trees of the Neon City, on the rotating wall of the Space Station, and again on the wrapping paper of the birthday scene.

In the film at The Land pavilion in Epcot, the woman testing the pollution in the Willamette River is wearing sunglasses that reflect a cameraman in a Mickey T-shirt. The greenhouse workers in the video after the farm scene are wearing Disney World name tags with Mickeys, and the farmer driving a harvester in *The Circle of Life* has one on his baseball cap. (You need good eyes for many of these.)

Some Hidden Mickeys are so basic a part of the Imagineering scheme and so vast in scope that they are only visible to VIPs flying overhead, or at least studying blueprints and maps.

Among the largest Mickeys is the one formed by the central plaza of MGM Studios, with its two little garden "eyes," the curved smiley entrance to Mann's Chinese Theatre, and the round Echo Lake and Brown Derby restaurant "ears" (although additions to the area have spoiled it a little). Others include the Mickey-shaped forest of more than 30,000 trees west of the Magic Kingdom; a triple-loop interchange off Interstate 4; and the combination of concrete and bush plantings at the Contemporary Resort, visible only at penthouse level. Look back toward the Astro-Orbiter in Tomorrowland from the Skyway's midpoint transfer station, and the building becomes his head.

Some Mickeys are very fleeting—visible only from certain angles or when doors or windows open or close, like the stars in Peter Pan's Adventure; the windcatcher over the beach house at the All-Star Music resort; or the spotlights that roam overhead from Pleasure Island. There is one on the glass doors to the private dining room near the back of the California Grill, but the doors are usually kept open, and the "half-Mickey" is not noticed.

Some are visible at third-hand; several of the resort hotel room diagrams on Disney's websites have been known to include such things as "ice bucket and glasses" outlines. The in-room promos show Donald Duck and two kids floating in swimming pools, with their ripples touching.

Some Hidden Mickeys are structural in nature. The Haunted Mansion's "stretching" elevator and the two smaller holding rooms that open onto it is a Mickey. The burners in the barbecue shops in the All-Star Sports and All-Star Music resorts, though rarely visible, actually touch. The swimming pool at the Contemporary South is Mickey-shaped, as is the one at Shades of Green.

Some people see a Mickey in the World Showcase Lagoon. Until Mickey's Toontown Fair was wedged in between Fantasyland and Tomorrowland, the entire Magic Kingdom was shaped like Mickey's head. In fact, it's rumored that from on high, the primary theme parks still suggest a Mickey-esqe roundness (with Epcot and the Disney-MGM Studios as the head and the Magic Kingdom forming one ear), but that, as they say on the Internet, is a contested sighting. (In fact, there are some HM seekers who become obsessed; one woman even claimed to see Mickey's profile in the map of Pleasure Island, but it looks more like Goofy's to me.)

Other Hidden Mickeys had to be "molded" into the scenery. The scrollwork around the second-tier skylights inside the railway station at the Magic Kingdom are Mickeys, and the scrollwork at the top of the Opera House nearby is, too. There's a huge "dent" in the Cambodian ruins of the Jungle Cruise that is Mickey's silhouette, as well as three "lava rocks" way back in the forest that few guests have ever seen. Two others are cut into the rock lining of the Splash Mountain flume. There are half a dozen worked into the already amazing maze of the Animal Kingdom's Tree of Life: if you stand between the Safari Village and Oasis Gardens, where the tiger adjoins the road runner, look closely at the mass near the tail; another hangs upside down over the hippo, and a third is in the octopus' tentacles. There's a Hidden Mickey in profile near the wheelchair path to *It's Tough to be a Bug!,* and others can be found in a flamingo pool along the safari trail and in a silhouette among the rocks near the lion exhibit.

There are three round-headed palms alongside the monorail near Epcot, shrubbery outside and below Take Flight, three rocks on the ground in The Land, and, in some areas, patterns drawn by landscapers with rakes. The moss on the tree supporting the Swiss Family Robinson's house is Mickey-shaped, and so are the carvings on the chair backs in their dining room. In the brick walkway outside the South Garden Wing of the Contemporary Resort, there is a darker shaded brick outline and one cut into the tile floor at the North Wing entry.

Some Mickeys are in the clouds—during the lightning scene at the Garden Grill, and in the postcards from the BoardWalk. A couple of Mickeys are literally in the stars: there's an entirely new constellation in the universe of Spaceship Earth, and the outline of Steamboat Willie is "routed" in the star map over the register in the Star Trader shop at Disney-MGM Studios. There is a similar constellation in the maps at Disney Outfitters. In Buzz Lightyear's Space Ranger Spin, one three-lobed planet in the Galactic Alliance appears several times; it's a double joke, because it's called "Pollust Prime," after Paul Osterhout, executive producer of the original *Toy Story* film.

There are several in the new "Walt Disney: One Man's Dream" attraction at Disney-MGM; one is built into the scale model of the fortress-like castle at Tokyo Disneyland, and the nautical signal flags around the lagoon spell out M-I-C-K-E-Y. The model of the Tree of Life has at least one, like its big brother.

In *The Timekeeper*, Mickey shows up in the planets of the "Space Collectibles Convention" and the "Recreational Rockets" sign; on a plaque held up by Jules Verne; and even, when 9-Eye returns to Paris, in a very modern-day form, as the little girl's silver balloon—just the kind of balloon sold in the park. Madeline has a Mickey balloon, too, in the French pavilion at Epcot.

There are spinning circles in the "Circle of Life" segment of *IllumiNations*. Another Hidden Mickey is in the SpectroMagic parade: The mirror balls on Mickey's float, designed to reflect just so in the mirrors, become a Mickey from both left and right.

Among the many in The Haunted Mansion are: the eye with the three "pupils" in one of the holographic busts that watch you pass, the setting of three plates on the ghostly banquet table, and on the Bible next to the coffin. There are repeated Mickeys outside on the upper right-hand "turret" as you face the front door (the side away from the ride entrance). The Grim Reaper at the crypt in the graveyard scene is holding a mouse head, a la the Headless Horseman.

The trim over the Traders of Timbuktu shop in Adventureland are repeated Mickeys. Some of the manhole covers in the Harambe Marketplace in the Animal Kingdom have pebbles that complete the cycle. There are three brass trays over the cooking area in Spoodles restaurant at the BoardWalk; some of the china there has grapes and cherries on them in that shape as well.

The Tomorrowland Speedway ride has a diversionary, blatant Mickey in the painted mural and a genuine Hidden Mickey, created by the rounded grille of the race car on the pedestal with two painted circles behind it. Of course, Mickey's Country House is absolutely riddled with HMs, many of them easy enough for children to practice on: on the mailbox, the fence, the door, the mirror, the wallpaper—even in the garden out back, where the pumpkins and tomatoes bloom in shapes not ordinarily seen in nature. And there are others that might be easier for younger hunters: on the boxer shorts hanging from the laundry line in the waiting line mural at Snow White's, and again on the chimney in the Dwarfs' cottage (the one under the flower), not to mention in the witch's mirror frame.

There are several in the overhead rafters at Conservation Train Station. At Pizzafari, there's a frog with a carved Mickey near the women's room door—and a leopard who's apparently changed his spots!

There are several in *Alien Encounter,* beginning with the hieroglyphics on the poles along the waiting queue: In each cartouche-like set, the Mickey appears as the sixth icon down on the right. Skippy the Robot is wearing a Mickey Mouse watch. (This might even be a double dig: As mentioned earlier, Disney CEO Michael Eisner himself sports a Mickey Mouse watch in a Disney-MGM Studios film—and Mickey wears an Eisner one.) And there's another robot with a Mickey watch in The Great Movie Ride in the next section. In the film that goes with "Walt Disney: One Man's Dream," Eisner is wearing a Mickey tie, though it's not hidden, just sort of OpArtish.

There are a lot in the Pirates of the Caribbean, too: the locks on boxes, the lamp bases in the treasure room, and even some of the shadows have ears. The ironwork on the base of the hanging lamps in the last scene are mini-Mickeys; plates in the treasure room lie in the correct relationship.

The Columbia Harbour House has a trio of ancient "world maps" on the wall, each perfectly round, and there's a Mickey-shaped island east of Australia in the Dreamfinder ride at Epcot. There are stacked barrels on Splash Mountain, a fan in the barn, a knotted rope in the kitchen, and three kettles hanging on the wall, as well as a profile stamped into the purple rocks near where the porcupine plays vibes on the tortoise. A Mickey silhouette is chipped into the street of MGM's New York alley near the locksmith's store; the gauges on Rosie the Riveter's welding torch at Rosie's Red Hot Dogs form a Hidden Mickey; and a whole pattern of them is woven into the carpet in the waiting area of *Honey, I Shrunk the Audience* at Epcot.

The Spaceship Earth ride is full of Hidden Mickeys—from the Greek's tunic brooch to the treasure box lock to the teenage boy's alarm clock. As Rome burns, the ring on the man's hand has a Mickey; during the Renaissance, a painter is outlining three grapes with white. But the sweetest of them is among the most secret: On the pedestal behind the sleeping monk is a book inscribed with the names of Walt Disney, Mickey Mouse, and various Imagineers. (Mickey's name is a subset of the game of finding Hidden Mickeys, and in much sparser supply when you eliminate the intentional ones.)

Veins in the sign over the entrance to Body Wars make a Mickey. In *The Making of Me,* the balloons at the prom where Martin Short's parents meet are Mickey-shaped, and there's a Mickey Mouse doll and a boy wearing ears in Wonder Cycles. The blueprint rolls are stacked two on one in Innoventions East. At the Maelstrom ride at the Norway Pavilion, one Viking in the mural is wearing Mickey Mouse ears for a helmet and a construction worker on the other side is wearing a Mickey watch; there are three red floats piled together; and three of the holes in a hollow tree trunk look extremely suspicious.

In *The Twilight Zone* Tower of Terror, the little ghost girl is carrying a 1930s Mickey doll; the boiler's gauges form a triple circle, as does one of the water stains; and the sheet music in the library refers to Mickey in the titles. And just before the second drop, when the doors "open" to the stars, he's in the sky again.

In the Marketplace, the water fountain's spray heads are Hidden Mickeys, and the water jets themselves sometimes hang in the air; this also means that a "wet" HM often appears on the concrete. In the Seven Dwarves window, Doc's nose and eyeglasses all touch; and the World of Disney is positively crowded—the tops of the columns around the doors, the feet of the clothin gracks, and even the "notches" for the shelf supports are custom-shaped. And there may not be a single innocent mural or "map" in the bunch.

The "doggie-bank" from *101 Dalmations* has an HM spot on its right front leg. Not surprisingly, Cruella De Vil's sleeve, which holographically morphs into Maleficent's, has a similarly-shaped bit of fur.

A lot of Mickeys are scattered about the hotels. The cards that explain the soap/shampoo dispensers in some of the moderately priced resorts have touching bubbles on the back, as do some toilet paper wrappers. The overhead tapestries in the Polynesian

Resort are a Mickey print; so is the carpet in parts of Port Orleans. The artist 'who painted the mural in the Caribbean Beach Resort's Old Port Royal restaurant confesses to adding 13 Hidden Mickeys to it. Many of the bedspreads in the World have patchworks, impressions, or even floral prints that can be seen as Mickeys. The garden outside Disney's All-Star Sports Resort—the one with a white columnar statue and two black circles next to it—the spots on the carousel horses in the Board-Walk, and the wicker sofas all have Mickeys on them. Some of the round wicker tables with three shelves are themselves Mickeys.

In the Port Orleans Riverside food court, the Indian statue has a Hidden Mickey on his moccasins. The piano in the lobby of the Grand Floridian has a Mickey on its back and others on the legs. The doors leading out from the Coronado Springs lobby have an HM, and there's a Mickey silhouette in the bus mural of the bus stop there, and a white one in the Dig Site pyramid (fourth row down, second block from the left). There have been more than three dozen spotted at the Wilderness Lodge alone, and we're not going to tell you a one. Even the Swan and Dolphin get into the act: look for coconuts on the headboards and wall hangings.

Some Hidden Mickeys are visible only at certain times of the day: streetlamps that cast shadows only when the sun is in the right place (like those on the bridge between Cinderella Castle and Tomorrowland), railings (some of the resort railings at Port Orleans and Old Key West), or fences (like the nearby railings around the castle itself). The light pole between the Mad Tea Party and the Tomorrowland Speedway also casts a three-circle shadow at certain times.

Some HMs are visible only at night: For example, if you ride either Splash Mountain or Big Thunder Mountain after dark, you can see the burning building on Tom Sawyer Island, and the Hidden Mickey in it. And as you're exiting Big Thunder, look back toward Splash Mountain: the top of the mountain itself suddenly seems to have a familiar silhouette.

The staff gets into the game, too; there are numerous reports of busboys, waitresses, maids, and so on who spray cleaner in three bursts and then wipe them into (temporary) smeared circles. A guest at the Polynesian who asked for some bubble wrap for his medical equipment found that in several places three bubbles had been popped to form the old design. Staffers who rake sand or even drag it in tractors frequently leave three circles for the first beachcombers to see. And sometimes when receptionists hand out maps to new guests, they circle important sites with pens—in circles that adjoin.

Even the Wedding Pavilion at the Grand Floridian is full of Mickeys—but we wouldn't want to distract you at such an important moment.

Hidden Ducks and Dogs, Too

Although Mickey always gets first billing, his fowl foil, Donald Duck, and his best friend, Goofy, have their adherents within the Disney family. So there are some, though not nearly so many, Hidden Donalds and such around the park. In The Haunted Mansion, Donald is on the back of the red chair that you see with the floating candle at the end of the long hallway and on the chair at which the phantom birthday cake is set. One Goofy is visible in the rocks to the right of the waterfall on Tom Sawyer Island, but it may be lost to renovation. There is a Goofy profile on the Cowboy Boots of All-Star Music's Country Fair, along with Mickeys.

There's an even rarer Hidden Minnie in The Great Movie Ride; her profile (more upturned than Mickey's) is above the gazebo roof in the Hollywood Hills mural beside the loading dock. Furthermore, during the *Jeopardy!* sequence of Ellen's Energy Adventure, the make-up artist is wearing Minnie's white shoes. And Tinker Bell perches atop the harp in Victoria and Albert's like Our Lady of Rolls-Royce.

Nowadays, there are Hidden Mickeys in films, too: In *The Lion King,* for example, when the monkeys haul Zazu up into the tree, they pull a yellow Mickey out of his head—but faster than the naked eye can see without the slow motion control.

In *Recess,* the first shot of the moon shows an HM in the left side of the crater. In *Return to Never-Land,* there are piles of cannonballs on-board ship; *The Emperor's New Groove* has grapes galore. The fish in Milo's aquarium in *Atlantis* have Hidden Mickeys on their sides. And in *Mission to Mars,* the outlines of the departing rocket, the radar dish, and Mars itself join to form a familiar trio. The most subtle may be the ones in *The Princess Diaries,* which are particular to the movie poster—gems in the center of the tiaras, and their reflections in the sunglasses.

Astonishingly, there are even Hidden Mickeys in *Mary Poppins,* which predates the park itself: a profile version on Bert's drum early in the movie, and a three-ring version, so to speak, using Bert's broom during the rooftop chimney-sweeper number.

More Games Imagineers Play

Incidentally, the Disney animators liked to play games, too, and often sneaked jokes into a few frames of film that went by too fast for audiences to see them. (Too fast until the age of VCRs, that is: Some very "adult" flashes of female characters are coming back to haunt Disney, though they're being more careful now.)

There is a sort of second-generation Hidden Mickey game that involves the latter-day animators, including the computer whizzes at Pixar, saluting their own colleagues. *Monsters, Inc.* featured a restaurant called Harry Hausen's, after the creator of King Kong, as well as a Pizza Planet truck "borrowed" from *Toy Story.* Also in *Monsters, Inc.* comes a very old-fashioned tribute lifted from The Haunted Mansion's crypt script: The crew members' names are atop the scare-scoreboards. And little Boo's doll is Jessie the cowgirl from *Toy Story,* and her closet sports characters from "Woody's Round-Up," the TV show within the same film. Finally, the Pixar pixies tipped their own hats by re-using a trailer from *A Bug's Life* for the lizard villain Randall.

This once fairly innocent insiders' game turned a little Grimm-er after the acrimonious departure of Jeffrey Katzenberg and the creation of Dreamworks SKG (as detailed in the chapter "The Mouse That Scored: The Michael Eisner Era"). In Dreamworks' animated hit *Shrek,* There are numerous jabs at theme park castles, dwarves that need rescuing, and even princesses "singing" with bluebirds a la Sleeping Beauty.

Another second-generation game references the films of Steven Spielberg and George Lucas, both of whom grew up as Walt Disney fans. (Remember that "When You Wish Upon a Star" is the climactic music of *Close Encounters of the Third Kind.*) Some are tributes, and some target serious modern-day movie buffs.

For instance, when the rear half of the plane that was used in *Casablanca* was moved to the *Indiana Jones Epic Stunt Spectacular* at Disney-MGM Studios, Imagineers drilled and reshaped three holes in the metal to get a Mickey into the mix. (Talk about movie pedigrees! The whole airplane should probably be bronzed.)

Pharaoh Mickey (and cup server Donald) are in the hieroglyphs of the *Raiders of the Lost Ark* segment of The Great Movie Ride, as are robots C-3PO and R2D2. There are several Hidden Mickeys in Lucas' Star Tours: One of the baby Ewoks is carrying a stuffed Mickey toy, and the first G2 robot is wearing a Mickey Mouse watch. There's also one on the phone directory sign in the waiting queue.

The hide-and-seek is beginning to spread beyond Mickey and the occasional Donald. Lucas himself makes a couple of guest appearances: Visitors waiting to enter Star Tours hear a call for "Egroeg Sacul," George Lucas spelled backwards. A hazardous materials truck has a registration number that is, or at least was, the phone number for Lucasfilms, and the truck license plate number THX-1138, the name of an early Lucas film. These are, in effect, the Hidden Georges; he makes an intentional appearance during the Disney-MGM Studios Tour as well.

Another, though less common, adult game hidden throughout Walt Disney World is the literary quotation, a sort of *Name That Tune* as you go along. For instance, the Greek being quoted by the classical actors in Spaceship Earth is from Sophocles' *Oedipus Rex,* and the book in the Renaissance section is Virgil's *Aeneid.* Birnbaum says that the type on Gutenberg's press is in fact moveable, and the page he is proofing is a replica of one from the Huntington Library's original Bible. (And since Spaceship Earth is such a literary treasure-hunt trove, the listing of Walt's name in the monk's book may also be an Imagineer's compliment, from the old poem *Abou Ben Adhem,* "Write me as one who loved his fellow men," Ben Adhem instructs the angel, and when he saw "the names of those whom love of God had bless'd . . . Lo, [his] name led all the rest!") The illustrations in the painted pavilion at the Kali River Rapids are taken from classical Indian animal stories, the Aesop's fables of the East, called the *Jakata Tales.*

In DinoLand U.S.A., as you wander through the skeleton display toward the Dinosaur ride, you'll hear such pop songs as "I Fall to Pieces," "Bad to the Bone," and "It's the End of the World as We Know It." As you pass the Jungle Cruise, you may hear, but not focus on, Cole Porter's catchy "You're the Tops," which includes the lyrics, "You're the melody from a symphony by Strauss/You're an O'Neill drama/You're Whistler's Mama— You're Mickey Mouse!"

Some in-jokes are almost like philosophical debates: the skeletons who are playing chess in Pirates of the Caribbean are actually at stalemate. (Would that make it a dead draw?)

There's one other type of hidden tribute woven throughout the park: what might be called "hidden flickies," or movie and TV clips slipped without fanfare into other sets in addition to the intentional clips. Many are Disney's own: *The Little Mermaid* is among the items dumped into the "brain" at Cranial Command; a hidden Pocahontas has been spotted in the newsreel at Space Mountain; in *The Making of Me,* the parents go in to see *20,000 Leagues Under the Sea,* which also appears in Spaceship Earth; the preshow of *Alien Encounter* has film from *Mission to Mars,* the show that the *Encounter* replaced; and bits from *The Black Hole* are visible at Dreamfinder's home. There are also the Lucas and Spielberg references mentioned above. But some are even stranger: The music at *The Twilight Zone* Tower of Terror, in addition to the familiar da-da-da-da, also includes the ghostly theme from *The Shining.* Heeeeeere's Mickey!

One great sight gag is at Pleasure Island—the rotating giant dinosaur next to Planet Hollywood: it's a dead ringer for Earl Sinclair, the Jackie Gleason–like *pater Tyrannosaurus* of the cult classic satire *Dinosaurs,* which cheerfully lampooned modern television and entertainment in best Jim Henson style. RIP, Rex.

Friends of Walt, both high and low, make cameo appearances: in the scene in Pirates of the Caribbean in which a man in jail is trying to sneak the keys away, the man next to the dog is Sid Caesar, and the white-haired prisoner is believed to have been modeled on a longtime janitor who often supplied Imagineers with ideas.

The last concentrated group of tributes is also built into *The Twilight Zone* Tower of Terror, and these, not surprisingly, are to the Rod Serling TV series itself. Imagineers viewed every one of the 156 original episodes at least twice—and most of Serling's introductions more often than that—before piecing together the video. And *Twilight Zone* memorabilia is displayed throughout the ride—enough to spark a new Hidden Serling chase among his fans. Some of the props displayed in the building are the broken glasses from "Time Enough at Last," the heartbreaking story in which book lover Burgess Meredith survives a nuclear holocaust only to drop his only eyeglasses; the alien "cookbook" from "To Serve Man"; and a robot miniature invader.

Incidentally, watch Serling's hands closely; since Walt Disney's lung cancer converted him to a critic of smoking, Serling's omnipresent cigarette has been erased from the film—as has a cigarette in the picture of Walt with Laurel and Hardy on display in "The Disney Story" in the Magic Kingdom.

Follow the Yellow Brick Road

Another sort of tribute the Imagineers paid Walt Disney was to embed his road map of the Magic Kingdom, however subtly, into the layouts of all three other theme parks. As discussed in depth in "America's Adventures in Wonderland," Walt Disney intended every guest at the Magic Kingdom to begin a visit by passing through the circuit of the railroad, the physical transition from one world to another, into Main Street. This same controlled passage is built into Epcot, only this time the palace is Earth itself, in the glittering form of Spaceship Earth, and the monorail loop replaces the railroad (just as the Tomorrowland Transit Authority is the "train" of Tomorrowland).

At Disney-MGM Studios, you still have to take the pilgrimage route along Hollywood Boulevard, which becomes the "main street" of the film industry. Here the temple at the end of the ritual path is Mann's Chinese Theatre, the site of all those legendary star-studded movie premieres—the Cinderella Castle of the silver screen. It was also the spot where starlets used to put their feet in concrete, if not glass slippers: If you look around, you'll find the imprints of Dorothy's ruby slippers right there.

At Animal Kingdom, you are drawn skillfully through meandering "caves" and animal pens, until suddenly that immense temple of evolution, the Tree of Life, is revealed, standing not quite so tall as the castle or Spaceship Earth but clearly the centerpiece of the enterprise. And as if to make up for the difference, the train in this park is a real one—the diesel-powered Wilderness Express to Conservation Station.

Also, perhaps as a tribute to Walt's own fascination with explorers and maps, each of the main avenues in the parks is laid out on a north-south axis.

There is one striking difference between Hollywood Boulevard and the other "main streets" in the Magic Kingdom and Epcot: It looks lived-in. Paints are faded, or rather mixed to look aged. Similarly, while Walt's beloved Main Street is immaculately, obsessively clean, the New York street set at Disney-MGM includes theatrical grime and even graffiti—dirt that has to be maintained just as meticulously as the spotless paint of Main Street. The Big City, apparently, isn't quite as magical as the Small Town. And the Animal Kingdom's main street is even more theatrical, with twigs, fallen flowers, and bird tracks molded into the cement.

"Once Upon a Time . . ."

After the look, the location, the levers and gears, and the special effects, storyboards still have one other essential element: the story. And although the scripts of the thrill rides become obvious, the Disney folks still like to have a fable for every feature.

Big Thunder Mountain is so named because of a Disney-invented legend in which a sacred mountain in Wyoming would bellow in warning whenever "white men" stole the gold in it. The town down the slope, Tumbleweeds, was flooded when rainmaker Cumulus Isobar got carried away.

Pleasure Island is the remnant of the resort estate of Merriweather Adam Pleasure, a turn-of-the-century shipping magnate and world traveler who was lost at sea in 1939. His no-account sons let the island fall into disrepair, and Disney executives aboard the *Empress Lilly* riverboat saw it and decided to restore it. (It is supposedly Merriweather Pleasure's souvenirs that are collected at the Adventurers Club.)

Typhoon Lagoon was a resort swamped by a you-know-what, followed by an earthquake and a volcanic eruption, which should have been enough material for even the dimmest Imagineer. In fact, it comes off sounding like a combination of *Gilligan's Island* and *Jaws*. A sign near the entrance tells the story of "the furious storm [that] roared 'cross the sea." Instead of the

S.S. *Minnow*, you have the shrimp boat *Miss Tilly* out of "Safen Sound." It got stranded like Noah's Ark on the top of Mount Mayday and periodically spouts water from its smokestack like a beached whale. The two speed slides, cut into the landscape by the "earthquake," drop 50 feet at about 30 miles an hour. The artificially controlled surf tops out at 4½ feet and strikes the "shore" about every 90 seconds—thanks to another cleverly simple mechanism: a set of holding tanks that fill up, dump the water all at once (creating the tsunami), and fill up again. The most intriguing detail is the Shark Reef, another artificial coral reef populated by harmless bonnethead and leopard sharks; free snorkel equipment is on-hand for a Peter Benchley experience.

Blizzard Beach is a sort of "meltdown," the remains of a failed ski resort on the slopes of Mount Gushmore. (You first have to buy that a freak ice storm dumped a mountain of snow in Florida, but then anything goes in this World.) Theme details include slalom like flumes and a chair lift that offers a view so spectacular it's worth the ride even if you don't want to drop from the 120-foot-high summit on your toes. (The slide is 350 feet long, and "passengers" top out at about 60 mph.) There's also a kids' training course with "icebergs" to cross, and so on.

Even the less elaborate set-ups have little stories tossed in. There is a wedding ring embedded in a brick near the exit of the Haunted Mansion, and various reports have it that (1) the ring belonged to Master Gracey (the mansion owner), who tossed it out because the "body" hanging in the stretch room is his fiancée, who committed suicide the night before the wedding; (2) the ring belonged to his wife, who found herself trapped in the room and went insane; (3) Gracey was a sort of Bluebeard, and the ring belonged to his "last" wife, who murdered Gracey and then threw herself off the roof. Incidentally, "Master Gracey," whose headstone is one of those at the entrance, refers to Yale Gracey, one of the Imagineers mentioned earlier.

And Chester and Hester's intentionally "tacky" souvenir shop in DinoLand U.S.A. supposedly began as a gas station, but after their dog came home with a bone—a dinosaur bone—they realized they could make more money on souvenirs and refused to "sell out" to the Dino Institute.

Disney also makes fun of itself, at least sometimes. If it begins to rain, the guides on the Jungle Cruise boats and the Mike Fink Keelboats often say something like, "It's not real rain. It's just another Disney special effect." And an *Orlando Sentinel* reporter spotted a pumpkin that fell off the table during a carving contest; it almost instantly acquired a barricade and a wry marker that read: "Please excuse our mess, this pumpkin is being refurbished for your future enjoyment."

Pleasure World

The Adult Industry

Basketball phenomenon Michael Jordan, Super Bowl quarterback Joe Montana, tennis king Pete Sampras, World Series pitcher Orel Hershiser, even Miss America—the famous "I'm going to Walt Disney World!" campaign has made it official: it's not just for kids anymore.

Walt Disney may have begun with his children in mind, but Michael Eisner is a certified Baby Boomer, with decades of self-indulgence and conspicuous consumption to use as a market barometer. So the vast majority of attractions, rides, resort amenities, and new programs introduced into the theme parks over the last decade have been aimed at grown-ups. Even those that were intended to please the adolescents and teenagers, such as the water parks and thrill rides, have been wildly successful among the adults as well.

It's the greening of Disney World—physically and economically—and in some cases the graying as well. You can hear it in the music of Pleasure Island (golden oldies, modern soul, and "adult alternative", the three hottest formats in modern radio), see it in the bars, and spot it on the massage menu. You can see it on the restaurant menus, too, although Disney food seems to be one of the few things Imagineers can't make better; you can certainly see it in the celebrity chef names taken from the trendy food mags Americans read by the millions.

You can measure it in the increasing number of recreational activities available at the resorts: golf, tennis, croquet, swimming, boating, fishing, skiing, weightlifting, running, rollerblading, volleyball, biking, even parasailing and rock climbing. (It's no surprise that the first Walt Disney resorts outside park grounds are at golf and tennis havens: Vero Beach, Florida, and Hilton Head, South Carolina.) You can see it in the superluxury cruise ships, the *Disney Magic* and *Disney Wonder,* that are cashing in on both the Club Med mentality and *Titanic* nostalgia. You can also figure it into the number of convention centers and executive retreats built into the resorts.

But, by far, Disney's biggest and shrewdest push of modern times is into the spectator sports arena. In 1992, Disney paid $50 million—half in franchise fees, half against prospective losses to the L.A. Kings—for the National Hockey League's expansion team, the Mighty Ducks (and $600 million for NHL broadcast rights). In 1995, Disney World added an LPGA tour event to its annual PGA championship and acquired the 24-hour ESPN sports cable network as part of its huge deal for ABC/Capital Cities. In January 1996, 50,000 fans watched the Indy Racing League's first Indy 200 race on Disney's $6 million, one-mile, oval track just west of the Magic Kingdom's parking lot. In the same year, Disney paid an estimated $140 million for the American League's California Angels and $70 million toward the renovation of Anaheim Stadium (now Edison Field).

In May 1997, Walt Disney World unveiled its $100-million Disney's Wide World of Sports athletic complex. A 200-acre professional playground, it is designed to be the greatest permanent center for amateur athletics in the country, serving as headquarters of the Amateur Athletic Union (AAU); the training camp and preseason home to the Atlanta Braves; in-season home of the Orlando Rays, the AA farm team of the Tampa Bay Devil Rays; and home stadium to perennial basketball faves the Harlem Globetrotters. It has since added the U.S. Men's Clay Court Championships to its annual extravaganzas, and a popular marathon that is run on a different course through the theme parks every January.

In 1998, Disney paid out more than $10 billion for rights to broadcast the NFL and the collegiate championship bowls that are the New Year's Day rituals of America's couch potatoes. Early in 2002, in a three-way deal also involving AOL Time Warner, Disney entered into a six-year agreement with the National Basketball Association to broadcast more than 130 games each year over ABC and ESPN, including the post-season and finals, for

$2.4 billion. Even before that, Disney executives had reported the company's sports programming costs at $12 billion.

Disney has also lured coach-turned-announcer John Madden away from Fox to the floundering Monday Night Football at a cost of $20 million over four years.

The value of these sports-oriented investments is incalculable. While sporting events on television in and of themselves are rarely profitable, they are unequaled showcases for network tie-ins and promotions. (Eisner himself has taken to making halftime appearances to promote forthcoming movies, a la *Wonderful World of Disney.*) And though ABC itself has gone into serious decline since Disney purchased it, the ESPN properties alone—six cable channels, a radio network, the website, a magazine, and the ESPN Zone restaurants—is reported to be worth $25 million more than the $19.6 billion Disney paid for the entire ABC/Capital Cities package.

So Disney knows sports, and even more important, Disney knows audience share. The BoardWalk has its own super sports bar/game room complex that is a virtual temple of the ESPN sports cable channel. To grasp the younger spectator and participator sports audience, ESPN has invented the Extreme or X Games, a cross between a fringe Olympics and headbanger videos. The sports-friendly ABC network also keeps track of niche audiences with its myriad baseball, Little League, tennis, figure skating, and golf offerings. Disney even built a family resort hotel based on the "family that plays together, stays together" concept, the All-Star Sports Resort.

All this bears the mark of Eisner, who has always seen how his own interests—in this case, both spectator sports and athletic hobbies—reflected Americans', just as the Magic Kingdom represents Walt's. Throughout his career, Eisner kept Saturday mornings free to watch his sons' soccer or Little League or football games. Eisner has been to the Indy 500 (that's where he discovered how popular both Jim Varney's character "Ernest" and stock car racing are; after returning, he commissioned *Ernest Saves Christmas* and began considering a mini-track for Walt Disney World). Eisner plays golf. His 1996 summer vacation included a weeklong bicycling trip through the Loire Valley of France. Walt Disney World is now Michael Eisner's park for children of all ages—the children of all ages, 21st-century style.

Adult Fare

The heavier emphasis on young adults is obvious in the food and beverage services, to use corporate bizspeak. After years of sticking to Walt's no-alcohol rule—the one that kept Walt Disney World out of St. Louis—Eisner's Disney World has relaxed it everywhere except within the Magic Kingdom itself. Beer is on sale on the "street" at Epcot, where you can drink as you promenade as if you were in New Orleans. The beers even match the national themes: Harp is on tap at the Rose & Crown Pub in the United Kingdom, Dos Equis on draft in Mexico's Cantina de San Angel, Beck's in the German Biergarten, Molson in the Canadian Refreshment Port, Kirin at the Japanese Matsu No Ma, Samuel Adams at The American Adventure. Both the German and French pavilions sell wines by the glass or bottle, the Akershus buffet in the Norway pavilion has Aquavit, and the Japanese complex has sake for drinking or carrying out. Pleasure Island and even the Animal Kingdom have walk-up bars, and there are shops at Disney Village Marketplace and in several of the resort hotel lobbies that have wines and liquor miniatures for retail sale.

Walt Disney World has even jumped on the microbrewery bandwagon, with custom-brewed house labels at the Territory Lounge in Wilderness Lodge, Outer Rim at the Contemporary, Fulton's Crab House outside Pleasure Island, and Harry's Safari Bar at the Dolphin. The Crew's Cup Lounge at the Yacht Club has three dozen beers; the Laughing Kookabura at the Wyndham Palace has nearly a hundred. The BoardWalk resort even has its own brewpub, the Big River Grille & BrewingWorks, with five seasonal recipes brewed on the spot.

The fancier restaurants all have long wine lists, and several have special tasting menus as well. Martha's Vineyard Lounge at the Beach Club, like the big wine bars in New York and Los Angeles, offers almost any of its wines in two-ounce flights. At Arthur's 27 restaurant in the Wyndham Palace, the private dining room, which holds up to 12 people, is really the wine "cellar," with 800 bottles on display. The California Grill has a very smart all-domestic wine list and a free wine-advice service; call any time between noon and 10 p.m. (phone (407) 824-1576). And though Don Shula's Steakhouse in the Dolphin gets more publicity, Palio's in the Swan, with a recently "raised" profile, has an often-underestimated Italian list.

Other recent consumer trends taken note of are espresso bars (including the Starring Rolls Bakery at MGM Studios, Forty Thirst Street on the West Side, and the Fountain View at Epcot); high tea (Rose & Crown, Grand Floridian's Garden View Lounge); and wood-fired pizza ovens (Spoodles at the Board-Walk, the California Grill atop the Contemporary Resort, Mama Melrose's at MGM, Portobello Yacht Club at Pleasure Island).

Disney has also taken to contracting with big-name chefs or franchising trendy restaurants with demonstrated market appeal. Paul Bocuse was one of the eponymous "Chefs de France" who designed the menu for the restaurant of the same name in Epcot (and now that the building actually has a kitchen rather than hauling in food from outside commissaries, it does the chefs much more credit). California cuisine star Wolfgang Puck has his own three-faced café (part formal, part informal, and one smatter sushi bar) in the new West Side development. There are not one but two supertrendy Rainforest Café branches, one at the renovated Disney Village Marketplace (where it replaced Chef Mickey's) and a supertheatrical version at the entrance to Animal Kingdom, where the decor and Audio-Animatronic elephants make it fit right into the scenery there. West Side has two other celebrity-connected restaurant-nightclubs: the House of Blues, a New Orleans–style night spot partly owned by surviving Blues Brother Dan Ackroyd; and Bongos, a Cuban-flavored café created by Gloria Estefan and her husband. There is already a Planet Hollywood at Pleasure Island and, since this one really looks like a planet, it becomes the "globe" entrance that matches Epcot's Spaceship Earth. And basketball superstar Shaquille O'Neal (who, it should be remembered, starred as the genial genie in Disney's *Kazaam!,* and who lives in Orlando during the off season) is a celebrity partner in the All-Star Sports Café at Disney's Wide World of Sports.

Some restaurants, such as Fulton's and Portobello, are actually operated by outside firms and pay rent and percentages to Disney. That's one reason most of the restaurants are accessible to non–Disney guests, i.e., Orlando residents, whom Disney needs to even out slow-season income. They're playing up the name-brand value.

Another bit of uptrending is the availability (and more obvious advertising) of "healthy" foods and special-requirement menus. With 24-hours' advance notice, you can have low-sodium, lactose-free, kosher, vegetarian, or vegan meals at most of the full-service restaurants. (There were rumors that the restaurant in the Animal Kingdom Lodge, the one where every room has a view of the live animals, would be entirely vegetarian, which seemed only fair; but it didn't work out that way.

But by and large, the new-look kitchens are just that: for looks. The official Birnbaum guide to Walt Disney World describes restaurants as "delicious," "delectable," or "delightful"—it's practically a George Gershwin song. The truth is, little of the food is first-rate. Most of the "serious" ethnic restaurants, even those in the World Showcase, are uneven in quality. The Teppanyaki Dining Rooms in the Japan Pavilion at Epcot specialize in a particularly Westernized form of Japanese cuisine, first produced in New York only about 30 years ago. It happens to be one of the better restaurants in Epcot, with pretty good teppanyaki (and good tempura next door), but it's not particularly traditional. Ditto Kimonos in the Swan; the food (some mainstream sushi, some tempura, some grills) is fair but irregular. The buffet at Norway's Restaurant Akershus isn't bad, but it's stodgy, smoky, and cheese- and mayonnaise-heavy. (Frankly, if smoked meats are your thing, the smoked turkey legs, which are enough for at least two people and only $4, are far better.) The Nine Dragons restaurant in the China Pavilion is notorious for its cornstarch-heavy sauces; the eggroll cart at Adventureland is no worse. The more authentic exceptions are San Angel Inn, a reasonably good Mexican (not Tex-Mex) restaurant beneath the "volcano" inside the Mexico Pavilion, Restaurant Marrakesh in the Morocco Pavilion, and the improved Chefs de France. And if you like fish 'n' chips, those at England's Rose and Crown are as good as most.

Celebrity status aside, neither Wolfgang Puck's cafe nor the Estefans' Bongo's have drawn much praise from diners. The House of Blues, surprisingly enough, has done much better with its New Orleans–style jambalayas and gospel brunch.

The only places the culinary staff actually recommend (off the record) are the classic-continental *prix fixe* Victoria & Albert's at the Grand Floridian, where you pay $80 a head to have every waitress introduce herself as Vicky and all the waiters as Al; and the modern-American California Grill, which has one of the only seven ultrachic Tom Shandley soufflé ovens in the United States. The Mediterranean-style Citricos and the modern-Floridian Narcoossee's, the other restaurants in the Grand Floridian, are overtaking their more conservative neighbor; and Palio's in the Swan has upscaled both its food and its wine list. The Cape May Café in the Beach Club, Fulton's Crab House, and Artist Point in the Wilderness Lodge also have their adherents, especially among those who keep their eyes on nutritional advice.

But these are still the exceptions among the literally hundreds of restaurants, concessions, food bars, lounges, and carry-outs. The simple reason is that gourmets, unlike Super Bowl or NBA stars, are *not* going to Disney World on vacation (or at least, not as a first choice). If the average guest at Walt Disney World were primarily concerned with pleasing his palate, the hottest dinner ticket at the park would not be the *Hoop-Dee-Doo Revue.*

So the quality of the food is generally beside the point, although the standards for purchasing, food storage, and preparation are extremely high. The restaurants, like the rest of Walt Disney World, are sets, part of the nonstop entertainment, either offering costumed servers (at the various World Showcase eateries), live entertainment (the 6,000 sea creatures who swim round and round the glass wall of the Coral Reef), or Audio-Animatronic distractions (like the elephants in the Rainforest Cafés or the entire Garden Grill, which itself revolves so that the apparent landscape evolves from farmhouse to rain forest to prairie). And dozens of the less formal eateries exist primarily for "character meals" and photo ops. Planet Hollywood, which has a restaurant existence outside of Walt Disney World, is a sort of memorabilia exhibit with fettuccini alfredo. Still, even it seems somewhat theatrical: Hasn't anybody else ever wondered what the star partners of Planet Hollywood—Demi Moore, Bruce Willis, Arnold Schwarzenegger, Don Johnson, and Sylvester Stallone, all of whose bodies are insured for millions—actually eat off that high-calorie menu?

Pleasure Island

In the Magic Kingdom, every day is Independence Day. At Pleasure Island, every night is New Year's Eve. Pleasure Island is the most specifically adult theme park within Disney World. Just as Typhoon Lagoon was built to drain off the market from Wet 'n' Wild and MGM threatened to overshadow Universal Studios (and just as the Animal Kingdom will undoubtedly keep more visitors from venturing to Busch Gardens), Pleasure Island, which opened in 1989, was inspired by the nightly traffic at Orlando's downtown club district, the now-floundering Church Street Station. (Orlando, incidentally, is upping the ante again by working on a huge riverwalk-style complex of restaurants and nightclubs stretching more than a mile.)

One admission covers the entire complex of seven nightclubs, as well as assorted restaurants and souvenir shops. The shops and a few of the eateries open at 10 a.m. every day, and visitors to Disney Village Marketplace can wander through without paying; after 7 p.m., however, tickets or multipark passes and hand-stamps are required. (Visitors or Disney guests who have been shopping all day and want to stash their haul before going club-hopping can rent lockers at most of the major nightclubs.)

Adults wear a plastic block-party bracelet that serves as an over-21 ID; those without the bracelet don't get served at all. Under-21s are admitted everywhere except Mannequins disco, where the state-of-the-technopop lighting effects, rotating dance floor, occasional pro-dancer outbursts, and shifting mix-and-match crowd make it hard to monitor who's drinking what. (There was an all-ages, MTV-style video club when the park first opened. However, since the real money is in liquor, and the majority of the patrons, whether in-towners or park guests, are adults, the club quickly disappeared.) Mannequins has become one of the places Disney cast members go after work; you can usually tell the trained dancers. And there are sporadic "outbreaks" of choreographed numbers and even featured performances; ask at the desk if anything is scheduled.

The music on Pleasure Island is safely radio-tested and designed to appeal to every susceptible segment of the listening audience. The BET Soundstage Club, from the folks at Black Entertainment Television, is a sort of two-story affair, with the deejays, veejays, and bartenders on the mezzanine while the dancers take to the concrete floor below. (We use the word "dancers" generously, though the club does have a resident dance troupe; many visitors are rather white, suburban, and rhythmically challenged, but to their credit, the staff makes no comments.) It has sort of a techno/house/warehouse rave look, but the tunes and videos are mostly hip-hop, R&B, and a bit of easy house—the sort of black music that advertisers have just realized most white teens and tweenies are buying. More recently, BET has experimented with bringing in live entertainment and the occasional celebrity guest.

Motion, the uninspired dance club that replaced the country-and-western stylings of the Wildhorse Saloon, is aimed squarely at the demographic smitten by MTV's *Total Request Live.* The dance floor is dwarfed by a giant video screen, and clubgoers dance along with music videos played thereon. The deejay is really a "veejay" here, as no music is played without a corresponding video, and a large percentage of the adolescent audience dances with eyes glued to the screen. Most twenty- and thirtysomethings are drawn to the recently renovated 8TRAX, where the music is mostly 1970s golden oldies, leaning heavily toward the retro-kitsch pop and disco; and the Rock 'n' Roll Beach Club, a retro but more classic rock and pop (yeah, surf music) club has mixed live and recorded music. The other dance arena is the outdoor West End Stage that treats the street as a club. Its bands tend toward—you guessed it—classic rock, although when the cast member dancers come up to the video bank, it may get a little more daring.

The Pleasure Island Jazz Company is pretty much what it sounds like—a nice, smallish room that offers really nice blues and jazz and even the occasional jam, but you wouldn't exactly call it avant-garde; it's more the quiet stormy, EZ-listening variety. Occasionally it has a name band, too, but mostly locals. There's a short, vaguely "N'awlins" menu.

The Comedy Warehouse is exactly what it sounds like: another of those half-improv, half–canned joke factories where members of the audience supply names and details and the cast invents quickie songs about them. It's clever enough, but with these sorts of clubs, if you've seen one (or the Drew Carey–hosted *Whose Line Is It, Anyway?* TV show), you've seen them all. Of course, if you like one, you may like them all, too—it depends on your sense of humor. Were you raised on TV sitcoms? Do you find recorded laughtracks infectious? By all means, march in.

One of this club's advantages is that it starts early—the first show is at 7:15 p.m.—and shows are fairly short, so you can kill a few mindless minutes while waiting for the other clubs to open at 8 p.m. or later. It also has the lion's share of the Hidden Mickeys in Pleasure Island, which is another way to pass some time: To the right of the stage, for example, the bicycle wheel "head" has a clock and a drum for ears; the trampoline has two drum ears; and at the far left end of the room there's a snowman whose eyes touch his nose. And on the dock behind the ware-house on the way to Mannequins, there are three tires hanging in familiar order.

The last club, which is actually sort of a reluctant favorite, is the most theme-parkish of the attractions in terms of theatrical experience. In fact, a lot of people find it the only Disney-ish place on the island, and it hearkens back to that old obsession of Walt's, the daring derring-doers. The Adventurers Club, as it's called, is a tribute to the swaggering explorers of the late 19th and early 20th centuries, half old-London men's club and half Ripley's Believe It or Not! trophy room. It's a little like a drinking man's Haunted Mansion: shrunken heads, sonorous butlers, macabre-comic souvenir cases, and photos of "members." Invisi-ble ghostly hands play the piano in the library bar, and a rather tawdry music-hall "gypsy" heads up a little vaudeville revue. There are costumed cast members wandering through the club, inducting new members into the secret handshake and the members' special greeting, "Kungaloosh!" And there are half a dozen different shows, each of which lasts a half hour or maybe 45 minutes, scheduled through the evening. The jokes here can be rather subtle, like the giant pharaoh's head that makes up one of the "stone" walls of the entrance (remember all those mummy's curses about entering tombs?); or cartoonish, like the casting rod in the hands of the classic statue of Poseidon in the center of the room. (The Adventurers Club also has a few Hid-den Mickeys around: Look at the "fallen" checkers on the far bookshelf of the library.)

Every night Pleasure Island, like the Magic Kingdom, Epcot, and MGM Studios, sends up a lavish fireworks display; here it's part of a nightly New Year's Eve block party, complete with "Auld Lang Syne." Last call and show time are about 1:30 a.m., and the gates close at 2 a.m. (Watch the three spotlights over-head; they'll touch periodically into another Hidden Mickey, visible from far away. And as you leave, look up at the Pleasure Island sign and consider Jessica Rabbit's quite pneumatic torso and her equally expansive hips.)

Disney's West Side

The West Side is Disney's best attempt to lure Orlando residents into making regular stops inside the World—not only for the rare family day but also for dinners, shopping, and entertainment—without having to kick in for a park pass. Like Pleasure Island, it adjoins the Marketplace, that super–shopping mall disguised as another amusement park; however, unlike Pleasure Island, it's always open to the public. (Some attractions, including the House of Blues music hall, Cirque du Soleil, and DisneyQuest, charge admission.)

This is where most of those new name-brand restaurant franchises have landed: Planet Hollywood, House of Blues, Wolfgang Puck Cafe, and Gloria Estefan's Bongo's Cafe. Two of the major restaurants here, Fulton's Crab House and the Portobello Yacht Club, are owned and operated by the fantastically successful Chicago-based Levy Restaurant group; the DisneyQuest diner is a Cheesecake Factory Express. Some of West Side's stores are also celebrity franchises, such as the All-Star Gear, a sort of off-premises merchandise shop for the Official All-Star Cafe (at Wide World of Sports) line fronted by rainbow-coalition athletes Andre Agassi, Shaquille O'Neal, Monica Seles, Tiger Woods, Wayne Gretsky, Ken Griffey, Jr., and Joe Montana; and the Virgin Megastore.

The West Side is trying to be a bit hipper than most of the rest of Disney World, too: It plays to the neomogul style with a cigar store, entices fashion wannabes with a designer eyeglass frame store, and has what may be the first New Age–style furnishings and accessories shop in Disney World. (Walt wouldn't have gotten the New Age at all; he preferred reimagining the universe to surrendering to it.) West Side has one of those elaborate celebrity memorabilia shops, Starabilia, and a retro-hip guitar shop, offering both cheapies and serious collector's instruments. It also targets the under-21 crowd with the five-story DisneyQuest, a sort of one-building virtual-reality theme park with interactive computer games (featuring many familiar Disney characters), oversized pinball games (honey, I shrunk the pinball wizard), "time travel," space wars, and so on.

And as if to emphasize the fact that Disney is back in the movie business, the 24-screen cinema near the parking lot entrance is state of the sales art, equipped with the George Lucas–designed THX supersound system, stadium seating in two-thirds of the cinemas, and even a couple of auditoriums with old-fashioned balconies and double-height screens.

But West Side's most ambitious offering is probably its most prestigious "franchise" operation yet: a permanent stage for a year-round cast from Cirque du Soleil, the Montreal-based acrobatic troupe that has revolutionized modern circus entertainment. High, white, and handsome, with multiple "peaks" designed to recall the real tents it used to work under (and which house absolutely up-to-date rigging and sound and light equipment), the Cirque du Soleil theater glows at the far end of the West Side like the ultimate fairy tale castle. Inside, its steeply raked seating makes for (nearly) perfect views of every act; the built-in trampolines, elevated stage sections, orchestra balconies, and multilevel trapezes return "tumbling" to high theater.

Even with its quite serious ticket prices, it's proved a huge success. Anyone who has ever seen a performance by one of the Cirque companies (there are now several) or its alumni spinoffs such as Cirque Eloise knows that it is gripping, thrilling, mysterious, enigmatic, funny, exhilarating . . . addictive. Even though the shows do not change very often (after all, they take months and months to conceive, design, stage, choreograph, and score, not to mention training and recruiting), fans return repeatedly. And with the constantly changing Disney World population, they will easily fill ten shows a week.

The BoardWalk

The BoardWalk, which opened in the summer of 1996, is a somewhat more sophisticated nightlife strip, or at least in theory. It's half resort, half theme park—the hotel is built right over parts of the entertainment and shopping strip—and the theme is the Atlantic City/Long Island resorts of the 1930s. Its attractions include a dueling-pianos comedy-music bar, a big band dance club with open-air dancing and a ceiling glittering with mirror balls, a brewpub, and an over-the-top sports bar, plus a specialty seafood restaurant and a trendy-fare Mediterranean al fresco trattoria.

It's half theme park in terms of admission policies, too: There is no park pass or ticket required as at Pleasure Island, but as at Disney's West Side, there may be some attractions that charge their own covers. And, as at West Side, both Jellyroll's and Atlantic Dance admit only adults—and are actively cultivating local residents as well as resort guests.

Jellyroll's opens first, at 7 p.m., and the two piano bangers immediately begin vying for bragging rights. Despite the name, which suggests jazz, the music tends toward the classic rock variety (again), but that does mean the patrons are sometimes lured into singing along. The decor is sort of speakeasy-roadhouse rough and warehousey, with stools pushed up against the walls.

Atlantic Dance plays on the nostalgia for the elegant dance hall, with a bandstand, a balcony to retire to between jitterbugs (and nuzzle in the loveseats), and terraces to take in the fireworks—complete with French doors of the sort movie stars used to step through with their admirers. Sunday and Monday are swing and Sinatra (free swing dance lessons on Sunday); Thursday is Latin night, with lots of salsa and merengue (and free lessons); and Friday and Saturday the club goes, of course, classic rock, with live bands playing what the promos call "baby boomer classics from the 1970s to the 1990s." Well, truth in advertising. Atlantic Dance also has a cover charge, but Orlando residents (or those who plan to return fairly often) can buy a year's pass that admits two. The club has some nice light fare, a full bar, and, inevitably, cigars for sale.

The Big River Grille & Brewing Works is pleasant, but the bar itself is quite small and the "stools" a little weird, something between a thresher seat and a shovel. The food is okay, though not overwhelming, but the beer, which is brewed on the premises (and some of which is cask-conditioned, though you have to know to ask about it), is good to very good. And it's a nice place to watch a sports event in the relative quiet of a regular bar, with only two regular-sized televisions.

Relatively quiet, that is, in comparison to the big bar down the street. The BoardWalk resort also contributes to Disney's elaborate luring of the couch-potato/armchair-quarterback audience with the frenetic ESPN World, a Sportscenter bar with maxi-screen TVs (and a 220-seat "den" to watch them in), another 75 regular screens, eight Internet hookups, a real broadcasting radio station, constantly updated scores and odds, interactive games, and virtual-reality pods. Hate to break away from the game for essential personal time? Don't worry: 14 of the TV monitors are in the rest rooms.

Of the restaurants, the better is the Flying Fish Cafe, designed in the fantastical style of the Dolphin and Swan resorts, with counter seats that offer trendy diners a full view of the grill, as well as table service. Champagnes and espresso, grilled veggies and steak, daily catches and desserts, copper and steel—you get the picture. A few doors down, Spoodles can't seem to decide whether it's a tapas bar (Cafe Tu Tu Tango on International Drive is a very hot Orlando hangout, and Disney never misses a market rival) or a pizza joint, though it's pretty good either way. Its promenade seating is either evocative (you might catch *IllumiNations* there) or incredibly loud (do you know how rollerblades and bike buggies sound trundling on boardwalks?).

Prime Playgrounds

Baseball may have been the all-American pastime when Walt was alive—and amateur sports were followed with affection and respect—but in the quarter-century since Walt Disney World was plotted, sports have become a veritable addiction among Americans. The only question is, is it live or is it Memorex? Are you a spectator or a participant? A physical fitness freak, weekend jock, cable channel-surfing champ, swimsuit contestant, duffer, or driller?

Don't worry. There's something for all categories here, and all carefully tailored for maximum fit and fun. There are opportunities to jog, bike, walk, or trail-ride. You can book a two-hour bass fishing cruise on Bay Lake, which was originally stocked with 70,000 largemouth bass who've been cheerfully spawning ever since, or you can hang out and stick your cane pole into the equally well-stocked catfish "fishin' hole" at Port Orleans. Not only can you get tennis lessons, you can play all night on the 24-hour lighted courts at the Dolphin, on clay courts at the Wide

World of Sports, Grand Floridian, or the Racquet Club. You can even get golf lessons from Gary Player's son Wayne and play any of five courses geared to your proficiency level. (If your handicap is your entire game, try the Lake Buena Vista course.) Or if your drives are really short, you can settle for a game at the two *Fantasia*-themed 18-hole miniature golf courses—a sort of spectator sport with legs. (Fantasia Gardens also has an exec's-night-out par-3 and par-4 putting course, full of extravagant sand traps and contours.)

If you're more serious, of course, four of the five par-72 courses are recommended by *Golf Digest,* and the Osprey Ridge course has a slope rating of 135—as stiff as those at the TPC Stadium in Ponte Vedra. For tour hounds, there's the Walt Disney World/Oldsmobile PGA Classic, which teed off almost as soon as the park opened 25 years ago. (Jack Nicklaus won the first one.) With the boom in women's golf, Disney World has finally addressed the LPGA tee, too; it now hosts the Health-South Inaugural, the tour season opener, every January.

Among the newer crazes are croquet (courts at Port Orleans and the BoardWalk Resort) and parasailing (the Contemporary marina). You can paddle, pedal, jet ski, sail, kayak, or pontoon. The three water parks—the small and sweet River Country baby bear, the mixed smooth- and surf-water Typhoon Lagoon, and the 66-acre papa bear, Blizzard Beach—aren't sporting arenas, exactly, although the idea of "skiing" barefooted at 60 miles an hour down 120 feet of water may constitute the thrill of victory and the agony of the feet. You can even scuba dive in The Living Seas if you sign up for the new DiveQuest behind-the-scenes tour (see the next section).

But that's all small stuff—small sweating—compared to the 200-acre Wide World of Sports complex, a more-than-Olympic development from the designer of Oriole Park at Camden Yards, the Cleveland Indians' Jacobs Field, and the Ballpark at Arlington (Texas). The $100 million complex includes a 8,000-seat baseball stadium where the Atlanta Braves play their home exhibition season games, followed by the AA Orlando Rays, plus four major league practice fields, two Little League fields, four softball diamond, 20 major league pitcher's mounds, and eight batting tunnels; a 5,000-seat fieldhouse with six basketball courts and a track and field complex; four football and soccer playing fields; 12 clay tennis courts plus a 2,000-seat stadium center court; five outdoor sand volleyball courts; and four lighted fields for soccer, rugby, or lacrosse; and a velodrome transplanted from the Atlanta Olympics, plus the All-Star Cafe. The fieldhouse hosts clinics and competitions in badminton, martial arts, fencing, boxing, gymnastics, handball, and wrestling—even groundskeeping and coaching. More than 25 AAU championships were played there the first year, and double that by the end of the decade—half of all AAU title events. The U.S. Men's Clay Court Championships are in residence, too, and the Harlem Globetrotters are here, when they're not globe-trotting. You can even take NASCAR-style racing lessons, from the legendary Richard Petty (or at least at his school). It's hard to imagine that the company won't look to draw serious competi-tors, and even dedicated amateur jocks, to special training camps or seminars.

All this may tie into another obvious adult trend in Disney development: the body biz. Most of the hotels already have health clubs—the one at the Dolphin is even the name-brand Body by Jake Health Studio—and several have personal trainers and massage therapists available. Then there's the luxury spa industry that is also booming. Many of the newer resorts have whirlpools in addition to the swimming pools; all except the studio apartments at Old Key West have whirlpool baths, and the "lighthouse" there doubles as a sauna. There are mud masks, facials, and body scrubs, and classes in low-fat and vegetarian cooking. What would be surprising about a Disney version of the Golden Door?

High-Class Fun

Disney CEO Michael Eisner was reportedly inspired to create the Disney Institute when he visited Chatauqua, a small New York town whose series of educational and cultural events, pro-vided for the personal edification of its residents, became the basis of a sort of informal annual tour in the late 19th century. He has also admired the Elderhostel system of offering inexpen-sive educational vacations for senior citizens at colleges and uni-versities worldwide.

But in this as in so many things, Eisner was following Disney's lead. In 1961, Ray and Walt funded a merger of two established schools, the Los Angeles Conservatory of Music and the Chouinard Art Institute, to form the California Institute of the Arts. It has programs not only in music and visual arts but also dance, theater, film and video (obviously, particularly close to the Disneys' heart), and critical studies. Now known as CalArts, it is one of the most prestigious arts schools in the country.

The Institute, which opened in early 1996, offered classes in what you might call home studies (a variety of culinary classes, organic gardening and hydroponics, topiary, interior design, gift-making), performing arts (storytelling, improvisation, script writing), media studies (radio deejaying or reporting), sports and health, and even Disney specialties such as animation, coloring, and sound mixing. Altogether there were some 80 workshops. Most were two hours long so that it was possible to take two or even three a day. There were two major performing arts venues there: an outdoor amphitheater that hosted dance troupes, acting companies, and musical concerts; and an indoor recital hall. Institute residents could start the morning with nature walks and t'ai chi sessions; major speakers and artists from all disciplines—Eugenia Zukerman, Pilobolus, Henry Louis Gates, Jr.—appeared at night after "classes" are over.

Unfortunately for its fans, the Disney Institute was closed down in 2001, initially just for updating and refurbishment. However, the rumor mill now indicates the property will be transformed into something completely different—either a revamped new resort or an annex for the adjacent Disney resorts already operating. The spa is the only part of the Institute that remains open.

There are other ways to follow Alice down the curiosity hole. A number of behind-the-scenes tours and educational seminars are conducted around the various theme parks, such as those that let guests in on the customs, taboos, and architectural references in Epcot's World Showcase (Hidden Treasures and Disney by Design) or landscaping (Planting Ideas, Gardens of the World); film and animation (Inside Animation and Art Magic); or the machinery behind the magic (Innovation in Action, Backstage Magic, which takes seven hours, and Keys to the Kingdom).

There are also tours that involve the real world: Wildlife Adventure: Exploring the Environment focuses on the ecosystem of a cypress swamp; Accent on the Environment covers

World ecological planning; and Epcot's D.E.E.P. tour is short for Dolphin Exploration and Education Program, in which participants become guest researchers in actual studies.

"I Do, I Do," Disney-style

Finally, there's the romance angle. Not only does Disney design (and promote) certain resorts for singles and young couples, they have expanded their roster of services to include weddings. Big weddings. The $50,000 kind. The mere idea may spell Fantasyland for some budget-conscious fathers, but a surprising number of brides apparently have grown up longing for lavish displays of long-gone romance—and what could be more ornate than Cinderella's own carriage and castle? As a matter of romantic fact, Walt Disney World is now the number one honeymoon destination in the country, and three or four couples exchange their vows there every day. (Which is saying a lot, since even on a weekday, all but a civil ceremony for two will cost $7,000—$10,000 on weekends.)

There are dedicated wedding coordinators who spend six or eight months getting every detail arranged, from the procession to the pixie dust. The most elaborate weddings take place in the Magic Kingdom: The groom rides in on a white horse (led by a lawsuit-savvy attendant), followed by the guests in open touring cars or trolleys and the bride herself in a fair imitation of a crystal coach, with eight miniature horses small enough to have been white mice in a previous life. The wedding is staged—usually after hours—in the rose garden below Cinderella Castle, and for an additional $15,000 or so, another fireworks display can be thrown in instead of mere rice.

There is a garden gazebo at the Yacht Club that is popular, but in 1995 Disney opened the larger Fairy Tale Wedding pavilion: a truly elaborate glass-sided Victorian gazebo on its own little island near the Grand Floridian and that also looks up at Cinderella Castle. There's a small arbor altar around the side, also with a view of the castle. Of course, most of the hotels have lavish honeymoon suites if you want to cut to the chase, and nowadays there are honeymoon packages that involve cruising to Disney's own Bahamian island as well as Mickeying around.

But don't start your honeymoon in the Magic Kingdom. For some reason, it never seems to occur to couples that even the darkest tunnels and rides in Walt Disney World have to be monitored for safety reasons, and that means some of your "private time" may not be as private as you expect.

Pirates of the Caribbean is a popular site for amorous couples who think they can't be seen and wind up giving monitor-watchers an X-rated show. Cast members assigned to Space Mountain have reported finding "slightly used panties, but no bras." On the other hand, lifeguards prize being assigned to flume duty at River Country and Blizzard Beach, where two-piece bathing suits are fairly frequently reduced to one piece. And there was a flurry of publicity concerning an Internet video of women lifting their T-shirts while riding down Splash Mountain. Although it was later argued that the film came from Disneyland, the fact that there was any confusion about the source is just as, well, revealing.

America's Adventures in Wonderland

The Disney Version of History

The Magic Kingdom represents Walt Disney's idealized view of his childhood, his creative philosophy, and his most devoted principles. Most of all, it is Disney's paean to America: the Greatest Nation on Earth, produced as the Greatest Show on Earth.

But the Magic Kingdom is also in some ways Disney World's most troubling theme park, because it presents a view of American history that leaves out more Americans than it includes. Disney World's version of American history is technologically the most advanced you'll ever see, but sociologically and politically it's decades out of date.

A. J. Liebling said that the freedom of the press is guaranteed only to the man who owns one; it is just as true that history is at the service of the historian who writes it. Disney, as pointed out in "The World According to Walt," saw the country in terms of the discoveries and the leaps of imagination that opened physical and industrial frontiers. Those were primarily the accomplishments of white Anglo-American males. That those same advances had negative impacts on African Americans, women, Native Americans, or immigrants meant little to Disney, or to the majority of Americans in the first half of the 20th century.

But while Walt himself may have the excuse of living in unenlightened times, the contemporary Disney organization clearly does not. *The American Adventure* was renovated in 1993. Walt Disney World's Splash Mountain, built in 1992, takes its Uncle Remus characters from *Song of the South,* a 1946 movie whose idyllic antebellum plantation and placid black slaves are not exactly a celebrated bit of political correctness. *(The Birnbaum Guide to Walt Disney World* says "Zip-A-Dee-Doo-Dah" has become "something of a Disney anthem over the years.")* The American history theme park that the Disney Company had hoped to build in the Virginia countryside near Washington, D.C.—the one that would have turned the Underground Railroad into a sort of "slave escape" thrill ride— was conceived in 1994. All this was on the watch of CEO Michael Eisner, who once helped launch the ABC-TV series *Roots*, which transformed popular culture in so many ways.

So before we enjoy the nostalgia and the artistry, let's walk through the history. The past, after all, is prologue.

Main Street, U.S.A.

The central symbol of Walt Disney's desire to mythologize the past is Main Street, U.S.A., the heart of the Magic Kingdom. In only slightly disguised form, it is the main artery of the Epcot and Disney-MGM Studios parks, too. Main Street was so close to Disney's heart that it is the only place in the entire World that you will see his full name written out. Stand at the corner of the ice cream parlor and look up at the wall of the second floor. You'll see, written in gold, the legend "Walter Elias Disney." So it's worth stopping here for a moment to consider its message.

In fact, you *have* to stop here; you cannot avoid it. The Main Street of Walt Disney World is the sole access to the Magic Kingdom. There is no other corridor, intentionally: Walt Disney wanted every person who visited the park to begin by walking the main drag. It leads to Cinderella Castle and to the other areas of the park. But Main Street is some sort of psychological requirement—the fairy-tale trial. Only after passing this particular facade may visitors enter their own "realm" of the Kingdom.

Main Street is the first glimpse everyone has of the Magic Kingdom. It is also frequently the last vision they have for the night, since Main Street stays open longer than the rest of the Magic Kingdom. It turns unrelated visitors into a crowd, a temporary "community," by gently funneling them in together. (It's only 55 feet wide, half to two-thirds the size of a real street at the turn of the century.) It is the site of regular "town meetings": the afternoon kiddie spectacular, the nightly grand parade and Tinkerbell's flight, and the climactic fireworks above the castle turrets. In the Magic Kingdom, every day is the Fourth of July.

But if Main Street is the first stop on Walt's Magical History Tour, it is also the first evidence of the custom-tailored nostalgia that characterizes the park. Disney World's Main Street may have been intended to evoke the Missouri main street of Walt's childhood, but only in the form he decided to remember.

Dirt was an inescapable element of those times: streets of mud and poorly formed sidewalks, sawdust floors, spittoons, outhouses, crudely painted signs (and even cruder paintings to accommodate the illiterate), fencing, poles leaning under the weight of layers of wires (for telegraph, telephone, and electricity), horse and cow manure, haphazard window glazing, or even open holes. Clouds of tobacco issued from every barbershop, stable, and food store, not to mention the tobacconist's. Railway stations reeked of smoke, coal, animal freight, sweat, and dung.

Not this one. If cleanliness is next to godliness, Walt Disney World is the closest thing to heaven. Walt Disney's Main Street is so immaculate that not many children have the chutzpah to drop an ice cream wrapper on the sidewalk. There is a trash can ("Waste Please") every few yards. Chewing gum isn't even sold in Walt Disney World, just to limit the amount of the gunk that has to be removed. The paint is constantly refreshed—the horse-shaped iron hitching posts are scraped entirely clean and repainted twice a month—and the architectural trim and details are made of fiberglass rather than wood; no fading or weather-beating is allowed. Brass glitters and glass gleams. Even the false second-floor windows open into rooms only about three feet deep that are carefully wallpapered and painted. Every fixture and piece of furniture is correct to the period.

This is no financially marginal Midwest farm town, but an old and moneyed community. The shops are obviously prosperous, and the square has not one but two "public greens." This is no place on Earth, much less turn-of-the-century rural America. It's Main Street to the max, with more columns, more gingerbread, more flowers, and more commodities than could ever have been found in one place.

All the jobs are "respectable"—no amenable saloon girls or pickpockets or quacks or con men. (And no castoff Chinese laborers.) There are no pool parlors or prisons in Disney's America, no doctor's office, no hospital, and certainly no funeral parlor. No school and, more surprisingly, no church. Barbers sing as well as snip. The horses that draw the trolleys would seem to have evolved beyond the usual digestive functions; any unfortunate manure that is exuded is barely allowed to land before being collected by street sweepers. In fact, except for Walt's own finickiness about such excretory things, you'd say Main Street was the embodiment of "spit and polish" decor. In Walt Disney's America, equal opportunity is not enough—equal prosperity and equal hygiene are also guaranteed.

Even before the fireworks you get the holiday atmosphere. The music you hear recalls outdoor picnics and town fairs: brass bands, barbershop quartets, player pianos. The air is redolent of popcorn, cotton candy, and just-baked cookies. The sidewalks are straight and the promenades inviting. (The "pavement" is a special slightly resilient asphalt blend, painted to resemble paving but designed to be easier on the feet.) The Crystal Palace, modeled on the showcase of one of those great expositions, the London Exhibition of 1851, sets out a banquet so lavish it would have fed the entire population of several such Midwestern towns.

There are evocations of several primary American myths, from the Founding Fathers and nascent democracy (City Hall and the volunteer fire department), to the democratization of "culture" (a theater and even an opera house); and from the boom-days bank (a working SunTrust branch) to an idyllic and preinflationary childhood (a candy store—Walt's personal retreat—and an ice cream parlor). And above it all is the railroad depot.

The railroad, of course, represents one of Walt Disney's favorite Great American Myths—the binding up of a continent and the "taming" of the Wild West—as well as his own first bit of personal conceit and the birthplace of Mickey himself. Walt had his railway laid all around the perimeter of the Magic Kingdom, had another built into Big Thunder Mountain, and had the monorail, the train of the future, run around the park. In his honor, there is a model railroad in Epcot's Germany Pavilion. But the Magic Kingdom station might as well be "Shining Time Station" or the Phantom Tollbooth: The route doesn't run on real time, or on real historical grounds.

Give Me Liberty Square, or Give Me Justice

Liberty Square and Frontierland are laid out along the canal in a way that is both "geographical"—from the Atlantic to the Pacific—and "chronological," following the westward expansion of the country. The Haunted Mansion at the top corner of Liberty Square is a Dutch New Amsterdam showplace. Therefore, the river it overlooks is presumably the Hudson River. The water skims New England, passing the Boston/Philly town square and the Yankee Trader complex and becomes the Erie Canal and the Ohio River (depending on which keelboat pilot you get). Where Davy Crockett's canoes pass, it suggests the great Tennessee and Cumberland Rivers and then becomes the Mississippi, where the Mark Twain paddle wheeler cruises to Tom Sawyer Island. Beyond that point, in Frontierland, the river might be the Missouri (the Diamond Horseshoe Saloon) or perhaps the Colorado. Whichever it is, it finally lands you in California just in time for the gold rush (Big Thunder Mountain). The various waters of Adventureland, which manage to mingle the rivers of at least three continents, are almost generic-foreign.

Symbolically speaking, Liberty Square is the oldest part of Disney's America. However, it only goes back to the British colonial era, and not even the very beginning of that, skipping John Smith (and Pocahontas), Walter Raleigh, and the first Thanksgiving (and Squanto). America is already established and mercantile when Walt drops in. The architecture of the main buildings of Liberty Square is Federal (Boston, Philadelphia) and Georgian (Williamsburg). The shops have clapboard siding or brick walls, white porticos, and neat signs of "ye olde shoppe" nostalgia. The centerpieces of this park are the Liberty Tree Tavern, where costumed patriots occasionally rail against the king's taxes, the Liberty Tree, and *The Hall of Presidents,* whose Audio-Animatronic chief executives are one of Disney's most popular attractions.

The first Audio-Animatronic "human" to debut was Abraham Lincoln—a Midwesterner, and a man whose physiognomy was so familiar, and whose reputation was so solid, that they made him a safe bet to win over the audience. He was the star of the 1964 World's Fair and remains a figurehead for Disney wizardry. Although he no longer talks for as long as he once did, he is still seated at the front of the stage, in prominent view at all times. He is also important as a symbol of civil rights—and, oy, there's the rub.

On the surface, the Bush-era version of *The Hall of Presidents* show is more politically correct, as far as African Americans are concerned, than its previous scripts. Actor Ossie Davis, his deep voice alternately somber and reassuring, has taken over the narrator's role. He speaks of dreams of freedom and national dedication, and the implication of his presence is that this great struggle for liberty has succeeded. But in re-editing the script to give civil rights priority, the Disney writers have exposed an equally clumsy willingness to try to make it all okay—and then make it all go away.

The first scene portrays the delegates of the First Continental Congress wrangling over the wording of the Declaration of Independence. The southern representatives, their accents almost insultingly exaggerated, are fighting solely to have the peculiar institution of slavery protected in the document. It takes the combined eloquence of Benjamin Franklin and George Washington to get the paper signed.

The next great icon of Disney history to appear is Andrew Jackson, whose near-savage treatment of rebellious Seminoles and Creeks and whose personal slave-owning are never mentioned. On the contrary, Jackson's famous devotion to the Union is portrayed not as pro-federalism but as anti-slavery. "If one drop of blood is shed . . . I will hang the first man of them I can get my hands on."

From there we jump to the Lincoln–Douglas debates, featuring that ringing phrase, "all men are created equal." If that premise is not true, Lincoln tells the restive crowd, then they'd better dismantle the entire sacred document. His audience—including what must be the most passive Indian in Illinois—is immediately roused to defend the Declaration. Nevertheless, the narrator points out, Lincoln lost that election, by implication because of his pro-emancipation stance.

But only a couple of years later, things have changed. Lincoln is in the White House and aging rapidly in the face of the gathering storm. Sketches of soldiers, all white: "Soon the blood of our nation was shed in a great Civil War," Davis intones. "And when it was over . . ." That's it. *That's it* for the crucial conflict that, according to this very same show, all of American history had been leading up to. Almost immediately we cut to a picture of the glowing Capitol dome at night—a picture that resembles nothing so much as that modern cultural touchstone, the night-time talk show backdrop.

Now the curtain rises on the parade of presidents. From Washington to Bush, each one is spotlighted and named by the sonorous Davis, and each exactly-sized and costumed president acknowledges his introduction by nodding, gesturing, or slightly bowing. The sitting president always has a speaking role, and Bush's speech is strictly tailored to the Disney script doctors' theory of enlightened American society. Now that "we" have such freedom, Bush reminds us, "we" must keep fighting to ensure the same rights for those—apparently in other galaxies far, far away—who don't yet have them. This must be reassuring for white middle-class spectators, but some minority visitors must find themselves muttering, "We who, white man?" (And that might also include the physically disabled, who look in vain for FDR's wheelchair; the polio-stricken president is seated tastefully in an ordinary chair, although if you have strong binoculars, you might be able to glimpse his leg braces.)

Yet, as you walk out of the hall, surrounded by fellow audience members who are, for the most part, looking moved and satisfied, you can't help but realize that Disney's conceptualizers know exactly for whom they script: The percentage of African American guests is very low, and those who do come, generally teenagers or twentysomethings, are not terribly attracted to that sort of entertainment. They're over at *Alien Encounter* and Space Mountain. The ordinary visitor to Disney World wants to believe that the Founding Fathers had only the purest motives for breaking away from Britain, and that the leaders of this country—elected, after all, by the right-thinking majority of citizens—were always committed to equal rights, and that somehow it is a reality. We know this because Honest Abe and Uncle Walt just told us so.

Frontierland:
From the Midwest to the Wild West

As you cross the subtle bridge between Liberty Square and Frontierland, you stroll out of the 18th century and into the 19th, and from the civilized towns of the Northeast into the wilderness. *The Country Bear Jamboree* is in the Rockies somewhere, and *The Diamond Horseshoe Saloon Revue* is somewhere between Tombstone and San Francisco.

Around here, the Native American, rather than the African American, is the missing link. Tom Sawyer Island is the site of an army fort—named, in a bit of irony he might not have appreciated, for Tom's open-minded creator, Sam Clemens. The canoes are credited not to their native inventors but to that noted Indian-slayer, Davy Crockett. You can buy a coonskin cap and take aim with a real, restored buffalo rifle in the Frontierland Shootin' Gallery, without ever hearing a peep about how white trophy hunters slaughtered the buffalo out of train windows for sport and left the carcasses to rot (and the Plains Indians to starve).

The only good Indians in the Magic Kingdom are, if not dead, powerless: the women, children, and ceremonially buried corpse in the Indian village on Tom Sawyer Island.

America's Progressive Adventures

The same selective editing of the national legend that characterizes *The Hall of Presidents* performance is evident in *The American Adventure,* the newer and in many ways more technologically impressive Audio-Animatronic show in Epcot. This America may be broader in constituency, but no deeper. It isn't only African Americans who are subjected to the patronizing rewrite of history here, it's also women, immigrants, and Native Americans. Those few who aren't omitted have been manipulated into serving the Disney script. This is sad, because the two animated hosts in this case are forward-thinkers Mark Twain and Ben Franklin, who begin by debating the progress of the nation. (Of the 12 symbolic "spirits of America" lined up on either side of the stage, only four are women, and they represent the passive elements of Compassion, Heritage, Education, and "Tomorrow"—she by holding a baby!)

Here, except for a brief salute to the Founding Fathers, the heroes are those inventors and adventurers who inspired the young Walt Disney himself, only reinterpreted as cultural boosters. Befitting this particular bias, our Fathers (like the rest of Epcot) have big corporate backing. "And now, on behalf of American Express and the Walt Disney Company," the host says with no trace of embarrassment, "welcome to *The American Adventure!*"

America is still "discovered" by the British (cue the sea chanteys), but it goes back a century further, to the *Mayflower*, and has an extra pure-minded dimension: The first immigrants are looking not for commercial opportunity or land or escape from debt—only religious freedom. It's a tough crossing, of course, for those poor seekers of liberty, or it is for those with the Y-chromosomes. (In the picture that goes with this *Mayflower* moment, all the ailing pilgrims are male and all the ministering angels are women.)

Thanksgiving and its native hosts are skipped over again. Once the pilgrims get to Plymouth Rock, they find no friendly Indians and no gifts of corn; in fact, they apparently find no humans at all, only snow and starvation. This is an "untamed" land, just waiting for the right (!) sort of men to whip it into shape, and they go at it with great determination. But soon they quarrel with Mother England and throw the Boston Tea Party. Mother closes Boston Harbor, and colonists in breeches and powdered wigs gather in fury around the tavern door. Among them is an African American, presumably a freeman, and aside from his complexion, he is indistinguishable from the rest of the wigs. Shortly after that, Franklin "climbs" the stairs into Thomas Jefferson's study and begs him to hurry up with the Declaration of Independence.

Always in a hurry. A quick stop at Valley Forge (which, technically speaking, is the most lifelike of the sequences, thanks to Washington's horse) and we're a nation, spreading across Tennessee and Missouri. Suddenly Twain, the subtle creator of Jim, the runaway slave, rumbles, "It seems a whole bunch of folks found out 'We the people' didn't yet mean all the people"— something most Native and African Americans had known for quite a while.

The second African American, orator Frederick Douglass, comes into animated view, but not, as one might have hoped, in front of a crowd. Douglass, who would probably have been lynched if caught below the Mason-Dixon Line, is seen rowing a small boat through the Louisiana bayou. "Even along Mark Twain's beloved Mississippi," Douglass says, "I hear the rattle of chains and the crack of the whip." And this tireless and eloquent agitator credits Harriet Beecher Stowe, the white author of *Uncle Tom's Cabin,* with making the coming Civil War possible.

When it does come, in a sepia montage reminiscent of Ken Burns' immensely successful PBS series, it focuses on a white family divided by politics. A woman sings about "Two Brothers," one of whom dies and fades from the "Matthew Brady" family portrait. War is over, again.

Twain then says something about "the wisdom of Chief Joseph," and the figure of the Nez Percé chief, the sole Native American identified in the entire show, rises into view. But his speech with its famous finale, "I will fight no more forever," is made to sound not like a surrender but like a conversion—an endorsement of the white man's expansionist vision instead of weary recognition of his greater firepower. Everyone, apparently, is eager to become an American.

Chief Joseph is followed by what should be a fun sequence: Twain, Andrew Carnegie, and Alexander Graham Bell ("Ah, the proud Scots!" Twain jokes) at the Philadelphia Centennial Exposition. It also features an Audio-Animatronic Susan B. Anthony. Yet again, her speech implies that the call for women's equality has not only been heard but already heeded. There, in 1876. We don't even need to worry about suffrage, much less an equal rights amendment.

Next up is "green" hero John Muir, whose robotic self argues with spraddle-legged Teddy Roosevelt on a peak in Yosemite. They are followed swiftly by film of flyboy heroes Eddie Rickenbacker and Charles Lindbergh, whose pro-Fascist sentiments are, of course, ignored. (He did, after all, inspire the first Mickey Mouse storyline.)

Now comes a truly astonishing sequence. It is the Depression. FDR is on the radio, and also in Audio-Animatronic person, talking about "fear itself." Will Rogers twirls a rope at the other side of the stage. And on the porch of a southern rural gas station

sit four men: two whites and two totally relaxed, familiarly jok-
ing African Americans (one strumming a guitar, which is at least
better than a banjo). There's no Ku Klux Klan or even prejudice
to fear in this America. We apparently never had a race problem,
any more than we had sex discrimination, underprivileged
Native Americans, or any other minority. Or a gender gap in
salary, either—Rosie the Riveter makes sure of that.

The last half-century spins by in a montage of photos in no
obvious order and with no identification. Among them are Judy
Garland, Leonard Bernstein, Bob Hope, Mary Martin as Peter
Pan, Eisenhower, Eleanor Roosevelt, Iron Eyes Cody, Gloria
Steinem, Billie Jean King, Bob Dylan, Alex Haley, Marilyn
Monroe, Johnny Carson, Walt Disney himself, Albert Einstein,
Frank Sinatra, Neil Armstrong, Frank Lloyd Wright, Elvis, JFK,
Sally Ride, and Mary Lou Retton. There is a sound bite from
Martin Luther King, "I have a dream today," but it rushes by.

Finally, a photo of the Statue of Liberty is replaced by a life-
sized torch on which Twain and Franklin are standing. So what
does Twain think of this brash little country? "I think the
Founding Fathers never dreamed of an America like this," says
Twain. It may be the understatement of the century.

The lights come up on the statuary niches along either side of
the stage. And look: the "Spirit of Heritage" is what they used
to call an Indian maiden, her eyes demurely cast down. One
wonders who was around to inherit what.

Of course, there are many other tactful omissions in Mister
Walt's neighborhood: There is Aztec-on-Aztec human sacrifice
in the Mexican exhibit, but no Spanish genocide of those peo-
ples, and certainly no questionable Über Alles at Germany. The
most poignant omission, however, may be the lack of a plaque
to identify the high Japanese harbor gate overlooking the
lagoon as a copy of the one at Hiroshima, one of two cities
destroyed by American atomic bombs.

Exotic Adventureland

The politically incorrect elements in Adventureland are at least
less concentrated than those in the history pageants, and the
Disney Company seems to have eased a few of them out in
recent years. However, the Jungle Cruise still smacks of white
civilization versus native primitivism. The spear-waving

Africans are straight out of a *Tarzan* film (Edgar Rice Burroughs' classic was published when Walt was 13), and the hired hands, the "native porters" also familiar from B-movies, are stuck supplying the sort of clumsy comic relief that Hollywood long ago abandoned. There is also a little egregious violence and the geographical convenience that the cruise route covers Africa, Southeast Asia, and South America simultaneously. You know—they all look alike.

The condescension of Pirates of the Caribbean, on the other hand, is turned toward women, although the mongrelized pirates themselves aren't exactly attractive. One woman captive, dressed to suggest an already casual attitude toward men, is scolded by her self-appointed auctioneer for "advertising" her physical wares; another is being chased by a drunken pirate through the doors of her home, cheery as a cuckoo-clock hausfrau. An official Walt Disney World picture book says, "While their victims may fret just a bit, they seem to be having as much fun as the buccaneers." In other words, if rape is inevitable, everybody should enjoy it. Disney's major concession to political correctness in the last couple of years has been to eliminate the scene of a fat woman in pursuit of a fat pirate. Score one for the heavyweight lobby.

Pirates of the Caribbean has been around for nearly 30 years, and it's too popular to dismantle. In fact, Michael Eisner has reportedly ordered a feature film based on the attraction. But the condescending mindset doesn't seem to have been dismantled yet, either. In the reception area of the late, lamented Disney Institute, several "paintings" purported to illustrate the kinds of adult classes and recreation available for registrants: cooking, aerobics, golf, and gardening. The fashions were vaguely Eisenhower era, and so were the stereotypes. In the kitchen scene, the women were cooking and the men were tasting. In the gym, the man was shown impressively balanced on the rings with his arms straight out at his sides, as perfectly horizontal as a model airplane. The women, on the other hand, were doing "spa" things, like standing in one of those fat-jiggling fanny bands (a scene also enacted in the frequently condescending *Carousel of Progress*). In the photography studio, the cameras were operated by men while the women pose. And so on and so forth.

There are African American figures in these pictures, but their faces are indistinguishable from the others except for the tinting, and their hair has no noticeable texture. It's especially true of female characters, including various dolls in It's a Small World and, more recently, Princess Jasmine and Pocahontas. Maybe it's time Disney discovered the world is wide, after all.

Corporate Confluence

It should not go without at least a passing mention that Walt Disney, who repeatedly fought to retain artistic as well as business control of his enterprises—even buying back stock from such essential financial partners as ABC, as soon as his finances allowed—might have some qualms about the widespread advertising that passes for corporate sponsorship in the World, particularly at Epcot. If the World Showcase is a three-dimensional travelogue, Future World is a throwback to the industrial expositions of the 19th and early 20th centuries—less education than brand indoctrination.

At Spaceship Earth, the history of communications is "presented" by AT&T; the Universe of Energy comes to you by way of Exxon/Mobil; Test Track (and its NASCAR-craze souvenirs) is the domain of General Motors. The Land belongs to Nestlé and Imagination flows from Kodak, which, like Coca-Cola, has scores of kiosks around the World. When and if Mission: Space gets off the ground, it will be courtesy of Hewlett-Packard-Compaq. Sega is among the gamesters who pop up in Innoventions, along with IBM. What's a conscientious consumer to do?

Admittedly, such attractions are expensive, sometimes prohibitively so, and no one begrudges Disney a little help. (The original Honest Abe, created for the 1964 World's Fair, was backed by Pepsi.) Nor was it likely that the executives of these partner corporations would be satisfied with having secret VIP lounges tucked away inside their attractions. Somehow, though, it does seem that such patronage could be downplayed, presented humorously, or acknowledged without being written into the scripts.

Frankly, my favorite alternative would be along the lines of the Rock 'n' Roller Coaster featuring Aerosmith—i.e., take a royalty from record sales and support all those other dinosaurs for a while.

Animal, Vegetable, or Mineral?

The "Real" World

Running the real-world systems at Walt Disney World may not seem as much fun as maintaining the Magic Kingdom, but it's just as complex a process. Disney World is so huge and varied that it isn't possible even for its agricultural staff to keep a running tally of all the plants, or for its veterinary biologists to be sure how many birds are on-site at any given time. All you have to do is glance around to realize what a huge task grooming the theme park is. But there are a few especially notable examples of Disney's green thumb and its lucky rabbits' feet—places to admire the landscaping and pat the bunny. And daunting as it may sound, the company does know almost exactly how much water there is in the World, how many lights are on, and even how many kilowatt-hours are used. (It's all on computer.)

There is one thing you'll rarely notice about your surroundings: garbage. Disney's waste removal system and recycling programs are also state of the art, and its recycling program is admirable.

It's Not Easy Being Green

"Poems were made by fools like me," Joyce Kilmer rhapsodized. "But only God can make a Tree."

Joyce Kilmer never met the Imagineers.

At Walt Disney World, trees are not just cultivated, they're, well, made—custom-tailored, cloned, and constantly relocated. Because of the strict visual requirements (taller plants in back, shorter ones in front, skinny ones in limited spaces), trees have to be constantly monitored for size and kept in proportion to the buildings they flank. Therefore, several "stand-ins" are cultivated for each planting—with at least one in the same stage of development as its model, in case the one on view is damaged or blighted somehow—and several other "twins" that are months younger. Replacement or new-character topiaries, those pruned and shaped tree-animals visible in the Magic Kingdom and around the Seven Seas Lagoon, may be several years in the making, so extra care has to be taken to ensure the originals thrive.

When the starring tree gets too big or turns temperamental, it is jerked overnight and replaced by one of the understudies before anybody notices. Some are moved to bigger quarters; the four trees in front of *The American Adventure* are in their fifth location. The better specimens among these overgrown trees and their discarded replacements are usually resold to area nurseries and often show up in full-grown splendor around Orlando golf courses and luxury homes; the smaller or less valuable ones may be mulched or moved into less visible areas.

Sometimes relocating trees isn't an option. In the case of Cinderella Castle, the plantings could not be allowed to interfere with the underground corridors of the Utilidor. But neither did the Imagineers want gardeners to have to fiddle around with the castle landscaping, the most visible in the park. So when the complex was being built, huge containers were framed around the "ceiling" of the tunnels and filled with a special mix. Then the root balls of the trees were placed in these permanent containers and maintained by spray hoses of water and nutrients pointed right into their hanging pots.

Sometimes relocation is only half the problem. Birnbaum says the lovely old olive trees in the Italy showcase at Epcot ran afoul of Arizona wide-load regulations on their way east from California and had to be cut to 10 feet by chainsaw. (The older bark is darker, so you can gauge the change.) But they survived to join the other imports.

Actually, Joyce Kilmer probably would have thought he was in heaven if he'd strolled the Walt Disney World grounds. The sheer extravagance of some of the landscapes, either authentic or theatrical, is breathtaking. Keeping Epcot's 10,000 rose-bushes looking fresh forces gardeners to start work at 4:30 a.m.

most days. On Tom Sawyer Island, the forest includes sycamores, maples, oaks, pines, firethorn, azalea, Brazilian pepper trees, elms, and holly, among others. Frontierland is shaded by maples, oaks, sycamores, birches, cactus, and pines—an assortment that you'd have to drive several days to see in real life. The Jungle Cruise, which encompasses three continents, combines trees from an even wider world tour—rubber trees, Malaysian tiger grass, bamboo, papyrus, palms, jacarandas, ferns, lianas, orchids—some of which have to be coddled with hot air from gas heaters hidden in the rocks when temperatures drop into the 30s. The Adventureland bridge cradles South African cape honeysuckle, Chinese hibiscus, Australian tree ferns, Mexican flame vines, Brazilian bougainvillaea, and dimestore spider plants. The three-story atrium of the Polynesian Resort is a huge garden with its own waterfall that keeps the air moist enough to suit even the tropically minded anthuria, gardenias, orchids, and coconut palms.

There are already 3,500 acres of landscaping in Walt Disney World, requiring about 40,000 trees and a half-million shrubs, and the numbers are constantly increasing—as is the labor and cost involved after back-to-back years of drought. Before the opening of the Animal Kingdom in 1998, Disney landscapers had to transplant and nourish more than 2.3 million plants and live trees suitable for African and Asian animal life on the 500-acre site.

Transplanting isn't always so simple, however, as is suggested by the story of Liberty Square's Liberty Oak Tree. The 100-year-old southern live oak, *Quercus virginiana,* which evokes the Liberty Tree in Boston under which the Sons of Liberty gathered, was discovered on park territory, but a good six miles from its current home in the Magic Kingdom. At 40 feet tall, with a canopy 60 feet across, and at an estimated 135 years of age, it was much too large just to be dolleyed free or roped and lifted out—the root ball was four feet across—so steel rods were screwed into the hardwood and used as hooks to haul it free with a huge crane. Once it was replanted, the rods were removed and the wood plugs that had been drawn out were replaced. Guidebooks say that nowadays the tree looks right at home, "as if it had been growing happily in Liberty Square since the Revolution." But as Birnbaum reveals, it wasn't quite that simple: the wood plugs became contaminated; the tree became infected; and a large section of the interior rotted. The plugs had to be pulled out again, the rotted sections vacuumed, and the holes filled with cement. A younger, presumably virgin *virginiana*, was grafted into the base, where you can easily see it if you know what to look for.

There are two other less striking examples of this massive repotting. One is at the entrance to Epcot: a massive three-trunk palm that had to be amputated into its three parts and then rejoined on the site. And when the BoardWalk villas were being constructed, Disney engineers rescued a huge specimen that clearly had a future on display. But, because there wasn't anyplace to put it, it spent several weeks in a temporary holding pen—the swimming pool.

There is also one tree that seems to have taken its destiny into its own roots rather than accept the Disney plan. The so-called Lawnmower Tree at Fort Wilderness, just off the marina path, either took revenge on an errant mower or gradually expanded around a forgotten one in hopes of hiding it.

But since the niggling details of real life—pruning, fertilizing, root trimming—are to be kept out of sight, not performed in public, Disney World often uses artificial plants in the seemingly liveliest places. All the trees in view on the Living with the Land ride in Epcot—which ranges through prairie, deserts, and rain forest scenes—are plastic, except those in the greenhouses. The most impressive one in the whole Land, the sycamore outside the farmhouse, is a molded-and-cast copy of one at a carwash near Disneyland.

Starting from Scratch

Like almost everything else, the landscaping at Walt Disney World is sketched out on the Imagineers' storyboards and then the plants are grown to suit. Disney World's main tree farm covers 120 acres, and the saplings serve double duty as water filters. Some of the less polluted waste water is used to irrigate the trees, whose roots extract some chemical nutrients and reject others.

In the greenhouses at The Land, however, an even more high-tech nursery is at least partly visible. Endangered species of trees, especially those that were once native to the central Florida sand ridge, are being cloned for transplanting to the Disney Wilderness Preserve. A large number of the plants used for cloning experiments at Walt Disney World (including those test tube–sized samples laid out for viewing by visitors who take the behind-the-scenes tours) are bear grass, scrub palm, and silkbay—all plants that were indigenous to the Florida sand ridge. A refrigerator-like vault with controlled humidity, light, and temperature dominates the room, and a photo collage, similar to an elementary school exhibit, shows botanists and Nature Conservancy volunteers planting these specimens back at the preserve. These test tube baby trees are also available at the souvenir stands.

(It must have seemed a sad sort of joke to the Imagineers when the Nature Conservancy overseers of the Disney Wilderness Preserve decided that the trees there didn't "look right" to the putative residents, and would have to come down. In order to restore the wetlands and attract wildlife, stands of long-leaf pines had to be clear-cut and other areas of palmetto and shrub had to be control-burned.)

Trees and shrubs are not the only green genes in this show. Disney is deeply involved in growing food and shelter crops in experimental ways: hydroponic and air-grown, genetically engineered, and in "closed-system" cultures that speed up natural growing processes. Drought- and disease-resistant varieties, vertically trained vegetable vines, and organically fertilized fruits are displayed, along with the cloned specimens and environmentally friendly species, such as the naturally blue cotton strain that will eliminate the need to dye denim for jeans. Many of the experiments are supported by grants from NASA and the U.S. Department of Agriculture, and, like all the pavilions at Epcot, The Land has major corporate sponsorship, in this case from Kraft Foods.

This takes a little of the bloom off the program. As has been pointed out by other critics, Disney never addresses the cost of building and maintaining such facilities in Third World countries, which are nominally the intended beneficiaries of these agricultural advances. Such programs could just as easily be seen as capitalism rather than altruism: ways of providing more commodities, or more commercial construction contracts, for the developed world to sell to less prosperous economies. Why not simply persuade the inhabitants of poorer nations to wear something other than jeans in imitation of American yuppies?

"I Went to the Animal Fair . . ."

On the other hand, Disney has been notably generous with animal conservation grants, especially in areas of high but endangered species diversity. In 1996 alone, Disney handed out over a million dollars to wildlife conservation programs in 29 countries, among them the Jane Goodall Institute in Tanzania and a breeding center for the endangered Sumatran rhino. Although such grants undoubtedly smooth the way for Disney's own acquisition of wild animals, they are nonetheless vital to biodiversity research.

"Animals" are an altogether interesting concept in Walt Disney World, where the most famous characters tend to have tails. Disney's animated characters are more folk than fauna, with voices and vocabularies (in the movies, at least) and emotions large and small. They are half-creatures, metaphorical versions of the centaurs of *Fantasia* or the Little Mermaid herself.

The full-length animated features—the ones with fairy-tale heroes and witches, like *Cinderella* or *Snow White*—tend to mix and match cartoon mice and "real" horses: The Cheshire Cat and the White Rabbit are cartoons; Thumper, Bambi, and all 101 Dalmatians (and their parents and canine protectors) are real; Jiminy Cricket is a cartoon, while the dragon in *Sleeping Beauty* is very real indeed. The real-life films, of course, use long-range lenses and natural settings with no animated characters at all. The 500-acre Animal Kingdom covers all the bases, with animals that are alive, animated, Animatronic, and imaginary (see later in this section).

Most of the live animals at Walt Disney World have been kept in very limited roles, so to speak. There have been petting farms at the Magic Kingdom, Fort Wilderness, and Animal Kingdom. Draft horses pull the trolleys down Main Street, and special miniature white horses are on call for bridal carriage duty. (These are, of course, picture-perfect draft horses: Every October, Disney representatives are among the 25,000 who gather in Waverly, Iowa, for the premier sale of Percherons, Clydesdales, and Belgians in the world.)

There have also been some unexpected appearances by alligators and snakes—as well as the less disturbing rabbits, ducks, squirrels, and mice—on Tom Sawyer Island. Cast members say the island's opening had to be delayed one day when a pair of alligators discovered what a good sunning spot the main deck was. Staffers joke that these periodic invasions are failed character auditions: "Critters can stay only if they present you with a valid World passport," meaning a Disney ID. The only animals allowed in from the outside are seeing- or hearing-guide dogs. All others must be lodged in one of the pet care kennels, and it's a testament to the handlers' aplomb that they've been left in charge of ocelots, cougars, and even bears, as well as various snakes, rabbits, and exotic novelties.

But by and large, the live animals are left to act naturally in and around the resorts, the undeveloped areas, and—at least for the immediate future—on Discovery Island. Golfers have reported seeing deer, otters, turkeys, bald eagles, and even some big cats, panthers, and bobcats. Even outside the petting zoos, just on the lawns of the resorts, there are animals so tame they feed out of guests' hands; squirrels, egrets, and ducks have all been spotted partaking of doughnuts.

At this point, Discovery Island seems to be in peril of becoming a Cinderella (Castle) story in reverse. It may look as though it's a rare "natural" bit of Walt Disney World, but it's another Imagineering triumph: It was just a scrub beach and hunting retreat called Raz Island before the hauling over of a few million pounds of exotic landscaping (250 kinds of trees and plants) and a shipwreck led to its being christened Treasure Island. Transformed into a tropical paradise, its 11 acres were home to more than 135 species of exotic birds and animals that, in typical Disney fashion, would ordinarily be continents apart: giant Galapagos tortoises, an Indian fishing cat, bald eagles (who are not, it seems, very collegial), ospreys, alligators, swallowtail kites, red-cockaded woodpeckers, trumpeter swans, Asian muntjac deer, peacocks, rabbitlike Patagonian cavies, and various small primates.

Its emphasis is on birdlife, and two of its presentations, *Feathered Friends* and *Birds of Prey,* showcased the tropical species such as rose cockatoos and hyacinth macaws; the endangered toco toucans and brown pelicans; and predators such as hawks, vultures, and owls. Discovery Island was accredited by the American Association of Zoological Parks and Aquariums and was the site of one of the most successful breeding programs for flamingos and scarlet ibis in the world. In 1983, it launched a last-ditch campaign to save the last four dusky sparrows living there by mating them with mixed Scott-dusky sparrows, but unfortunately the effort failed when a storm swept through the park in 1989 and killed the last of the hybrids. Discovery Island also had a veterinary hospice for injured animals like the one Conservation Station, as well as a wild-release training center.

On April 8, 1999, however, exactly 25 years after its opening, Discovery Island was closed to the public. Disney officials moved many of the animals to the Animal Kingdom, which has a much more extensive veterinary complex, but a great many others were transferred to zoos or private collections.

At press time, the company still had not announced what the island would be used for in the future. Post-9/11 cutbacks forced Disney executives to consider turning the island into a bird sanctuary, which would, paradoxically, require undoing much of the previous work: removing all the buildings, for example, including the bird cages used for emergency care and controlled breeding. The island would also need to be rezoned as "agricultural," which would ultimately allow for a tax break but would also require Disney to remove much of the expensive but non-native landscaping. Other possible scenarios have reportedly included going back to the Treasure Island theme and setting up day-long treasure hunts for families or groups; building luxury honeymoon cottages; or even building a Lion King–themed Camp Hakuna Matata (the famous "no worries" slogan).

Of course, the entire corporate mindset changed when the company decided to build the Animal Kingdom. Not only would the animals be live, the plants would have to be real, because for many animals, as mentioned earlier, the scenery is on the grocery list.

Among the animals in the Africa region of the Animal Kingdom are lions and elephants; zebras and okapi; ostriches and flamingos; storks and Egyptian geese; giraffes, wildebeests and gazelles, elands and oryxes; kudus and antelope; crocodiles; black rhino and white rhino; gorillas and baboons; warthogs; and an entire aviary of tropical birds. The *Flights of Wonder* trained bird show includes bald eagles, hawks, and owls. In the Maharaja Jungle Trek are Komodo dragons, one of the several endangered species being bred here, tapirs, tigers, blackbuck and Eldt's deer, banteng, large fruit bats, and more than 50 varieties of birds. Elsewhere in Asia are geckos, gibbons, mynahs, and other birds. That *Enchanted Tiki Birds* show in the Magic Kingdom looks really dull by comparison.

And unlike the animals in most of the rest of the World, Animal Kingdom's denizens had to be given as much real space as possible in an artificial nature park. (Although that sounds like an oxymoron, it's really what this is. The Animal Kingdom is usually referred to as a theme park, but it is in the vanguard of the modern zoo movement because as the true natural habitat continues to shrink, more and more species will only survive because of human breeding and preservation techniques—i.e., nature parks.) The visible veterinary operations at Conservation Station are only the beginning of the work required to keep Disney's animals safe and healthy, and some of the work being done there has advanced zoo science elsewhere as well.

Although Disney brought in many environmental scientists and veterinary experts to advise them in the creation of the Animal Kingdom, there have been casualties among the animals and protests by animal rights groups. However, early populations of park and even preserve animals are susceptible to injury and illness, and very few of the problems seem to have been the result of any neglect on the part of cast members.

Disney Wilderness Preserve: The Great Land Swap

During the original planning for Walt Disney World, the ecological engineers found a half-dozen different ecosystems, including a 7,500-acre cypress swamp that is now a wildlife refuge and the site of in-depth studies of plant groupings, symbiotic ecosettings, and water management. "Ninety percent of the scrub habitat has been lost to agriculture and urbanization," says one agricultural botanist at The Land, without necessarily pointing out that Disney has been the region's largest developer.

But without actually calling it restitution, the Disney corporation has at least begun a massive restoration effort.

In 1992, Disney made an historical agreement with federal and state environmental officials. In return for its being allowed to bulldoze and develop 550 acres of wetlands during the building of its model town Celebration, Disney purchased an ecologically important preserve of 8,500 acres about 15 miles south on the Osceola-Polk county border called the Walker Ranch, and then turned it over (along with $8 million to establish a trust fund) to the Nature Conservancy for restoration and maintenance. The idea was to return the area to the condition it was in 500 years ago, before the European explorers arrived, which meant somehow reversing nearly a century of excessive drainage, clear-cutting, cattle grazing, and even turpentine distilleries. Whole sections of introduced vegetation would have to be burned, fences and roads turned under, and grasslands and swamp reintroduced.

It was a good deal for both sides. From the environmental point of view, the Walker Ranch was desirable because it held the highest concentration of nesting bald eagles in the southeast, along with stable populations of wood storks, scrub jays, herons, ibis, fox squirrels, bobcats, indigo snakes, and gopher tortoises. It also hosted rare southeastern kestrels and Audubon's crested caracara. It was a good deal for Disney because it spent less than $40 million—$20 million to the previous developer, $9 million to the Nature Conservancy for restoration and a maintenance endowment, and about $11 million for research and permit reconciliation—instead of what might have been a great deal more in wetlands construction permits and waiver hearings.

The agreement turned out to be such a public relations boon, as well as such smart development planning, that Disney World's rival, the Universal Studios park, shortly thereafter made a similar deal to restore and preserve another 270 acres that adjoined the Walker Ranch. State and federal regulators agreed because the value of having a single large preserve is many times greater than having piecemeal wetlands constantly threatened on the margins. That deal freed Universal to begin its huge second phase alongside Interstate 4 on a tract that had included wetlands. The Greater Orlando Aviation Authority negotiated a similar land swap in the same area.

Renamed the Disney Wilderness Preserve, and now totaling 11,000 acres, the Walker Ranch area includes piney flats, prairies, cypress swamp (home to rare Florida black bears and panthers), and bay swamp. It's also a test site for the introduction of cloned indigenous plant species, mentioned earlier.

Like Discovery Island, the Wilderness Preserve has had its share of unwanted residents. Wild pigs that were rooting up delicate plants and reproducing too rapidly for ordinary control had to be trapped and killed by security forces under reluctant Nature Conservancy orders. These were not cute Piglet types, but 400-pound crashing boars, so to speak. Besides, they weren't indigenous to the area, but 16th-century ingrates brought along by the pork-hungry Spanish. Once slaughtered, they were left to feed the raptors.

The Park Jurassic Park Built

Disney World's largest theme park would have been called the Wild Kingdom if Mutual of Omaha hadn't found that a little too close to its own famous TV show title. But when Disney's Animal Kingdom, as it is now simply known, opened in 1998, it was five times the size of the Magic Kingdom, with a 14-story Tree of Life for a castle. It has already been the target of protests by PETA (People for the Ethical Treatment of Animals), but Disney, in a typically clever preemptive PR strike, hired animal specialists and conservationists and enlisted the tentative support of the ASPCA and the Florida Audubon Society for the project. The director of animal operations is Rick Barongi, former curator of mammals at the highly regarded San Diego Zoo, who says the "foundation of the park is conservation ethics." Indeed, at various points around the park you will see jars and brochures for the Disney Wildlife Conservation Fund, along with piles of the Rainforest Cafe foods and beauty supplies that partly benefit Third World countries. Disney advertises its commitment to conservation at every opportunity.

The Animal Kingdom is divided into three themed areas, each with some sort of thrill ride—something like a modern Adventureland, only vastly spread out. One area is the real-life safari park, with herds of Asian and African live animals—

including giraffes, hippos, and elephants—in carefully reconstructed habitats representing rain forests, plains, and savannah.

The African adventure begins when the jeep guide promises to show visitors a mammoth mother elephant named Big Red; moments later, alerted by a radio call from police in an airplane overhead, the jeep comes upon Big Red's "corpse" and a group of poachers, who flee as the jeep approaches. A whirlwind chase ensues and the poachers are, of course, captured and presumably punished.

One of the background soundtracks along the Kali River Rapids ride is a "radio broadcast" similarly warning of an illegal logging operation. But there is also a real "backstage" conservation station where visitors can learn about breeding, research, and on-site veterinary work.

The Beastly Kingdom, currently languishing in development, reportedly will be a mythical forest populated by dragons, unicorns, and other fabulous creatures (the new Fantasyland). Since Disney has produced a series of remarkably realistic dragons, from *Sleeping Beauty* to *Dragonslayer* (and most recently, *Reign of Fire*), they should be pretty impressive.

But even they may pale next to the Audio-Animatronic dinosaurs that wander the ancient landscape of DinoLand U.S.A., a re-creation of Cretaceous-period Earth. More sophisticated than the prehistoric denizens of the Universe of Energy ride at Epcot or the even older ones in Spaceship Earth, which are direct tributes to the "Rite of Spring" segment of *Fantasia,* these dinosaurs set new standards for realism—expectations that have to be pretty high in the era of velociraptors. (And let's be frank: It didn't hurt Disney plans that *Jurassic Park* and its sequels were monster hits.) The thrill ride here, Dinosaur (previously called Countdown to Extinction—another nudge of conservationism), climaxes in another simulated chase of the guests by *T. rex.* Disney's dinosaur mania most recently culminated in the TV-event-turned series *Dinotopia.*

As if that weren't enough, the bones of a real *T. rex,* the one nicknamed "Sue," are being preserved at another see-through laboratory at DinoLand U.S.A. The majority of the dinosaur skeletons there, however, are only half-real—casts of true fossils.

Ironically, while clearing the 500-acre tract, Disney Development Company unexpectedly stumbled upon some ancient animals already there. The first were gopher tortoises, unobtrusive types who dig deep burrows other animals then move into. Though not endangered, they are classified as a species of special concern. As part of the Walker Ranch deal that allowed Disney to develop its own wetlands, conservation officials also told Disney it would be allowed to wipe out as many as 2,300 tortoises over 20 years. However, many of the slow-moving residents were already suffering from an upper respiratory illness that causes runny noses, watery eyes, and coughing. Although it sounds something like a human cold, it is more dangerous, and a similar ailment has killed large numbers of endangered desert tortoises out west. Therefore, Disney decided to give as many of the gopher tortoises as it could capture, along with $700,000 in research funds, to the University of Florida.

In 1994, Disney Development Company found that the same area was also home to skinks, tiny lizards who lived in central Florida thousands of years ago. So it transplanted 22 acres of sand hill terrain, 6–12 inches deep, in a unique effort to re-create an entire habitat, and then repatriated 200 skinks. The 22 acres, taken to the western edge of Disney property, have been marked off into one-acre lots, in order for researchers to gauge the skinks' adaptability to other environments.

Earth, Air, Fire, and Water

As large a project as it was, carving out Seven Seas Lagoon was only a part of the great dredging program that building Walt Disney World required. Under natural circumstances, the Reedy Creek district would have been three-quarters inundated by water in the summer and one-quarter in winter. Most of the property was at least permanently damp. So, like that other Creator, Disney World's makers first had to divide the waters from the land, and they had to make sure they stayed divided. That meant relocating 9 million cubic yards of dirt—enough to rebuild the Meadowlands sports complex in New Jersey three times over—and carving out 55 miles of canals.

The water levels then had to be regulated. At the same time, however, Imagineers had to be careful not to contaminate, concentrate, or drain away water from land that had already been disastrously overdrained in many nearby areas. The water reclamation system designed by the Imagineers involved not only the canals but miles and miles of levees and a series of innovative water control gates—entirely mechanical in nature, so that no electrical wiring or human intrusion is required—that serve as "locks" to keep the water in the canals and rivers within desirable limits. It even restricts flooding during periods of heavy rain and hurricane weather. Since the late 1970s the water flow has been monitored by a satellite in stationary orbit using radio telemetry.

The naturally swampy conditions continue to make life a little difficult from time to time. Pleasure Island opened a year later than originally scheduled and its original $30-million budget nearly tripled, because the "island" kept sinking. More recently, a resort hotel that was to have been built near the Contemporary had to be abandoned because of soft earth.

And the Imagineers didn't just have to make new lakes; they had to remake Bay Lake—the little blue gem that had persuaded Walt to buy the land in the first place—by draining it, dredging the white sand clean, and refilling it. Joe Potter's engineers created tides as well, by installing a computerized wavemaker that produced a seemingly natural range of ripples from a few inches to four feet high. Just imagine what Walt would have said if he'd known that.

Nor was that the end of it. When it came time to build Epcot, the engineers had to haul the earthmovers out of mothballs to dredge another 6 million cubic yards of dirt to keep the World Showcase Lagoon down—it was a massive sinkhole—and the rest of the park "up."

Unfortunately, in recent years, the drop in rainfall (among other factors) has caused periodic bacterial blooming that makes the lakewater unsuitable for swimming; not a hardship in a park with so many swimming pools and water attractions, but nevertheless embarrassing. Even sadder, River Country, the oldest and by far the least "sophisticated" of the water parks (and the only one which uses recycled lake water) has come under the dual burdens of undesirable chemical balancing and dropping attendance. At press time, River Country was closed, and rumors among cast members indicated it might not reopen.

The Kingdom and the Power

Walt Disney's determination to have a spotlessly clean prototype of a park placed extra pressure on Imagineers to create an effective and virtually invisible waste management system. Part of the problem of littering was solved by reinventing the street sweeper: *Mary Poppins*–era types with long pushbrooms. (I have a special respect for these often overlooked laborers. As a small child, I got lost in Disneyland, and remembering the "Missing Children" sign on Town Hall, I approached a street sweeper in tears asking for directions. He kindly altered his brushing route to lead me there, telling stories in character the whole way.)

The commercial trash problem in the Magic Kingdom and at the Contemporary Resort, part of the original construction, was solved by the Swedish AVAC (automated vacuum-assisted collection) system built into the Utilidor, which is capable of swallowing 50 tons a day. Disney employees take the liner bags from the trash cans to the pneumatic AVAC tubes that suck the bags in and hurl them out, at an estimated 60 miles per hour, to a central collection point. The garbage is compacted there and then trucked to a blast-furnace incinerator.

There is even garbage disposal in reverse—a sort of recycling that might be thought of as garbage dispersal. For instance, it is said that the Haunted Mansion somehow loses rather than gathers dust, and has to have as much as five gallons gently de-vacuumed at a time. By one estimate, cast members have put down enough atmospheric dust to have filled the mansion to its very turrets, which presumably says something about the air purification system.

And there's the even more basic form of recycling: Every day, the inhabitants of the Animal Kingdom alone produce 1,600 tons of manure, of which at least part is composted back into the various parks.

By experimenting and adjusting its methods over the years, Disney has managed to integrate some progressive methods into its wastewater management, and to integrate that with its solid waste treatment and power production as well. The sewage facility is so efficient that when the treated and chlorinated water is released, it nearly meets federal drinking water standards. Some of it is used to irrigate the golf courses and wildlife areas. Some of the treated water is used to irrigate the 150-acre Living Filter Tree Farm, which is just what it says: a natural filtration system. (The roots and sand layer absorb certain minerals from the water before it sinks through the earth back into the groundwater.) And some of the water is used to spray exhaust at the incinerator to capture ash. The ash is then recycled again through the sewage plant, where it serves as a filter, and eventually it is mixed with sludge from the sewage plant and used as fertilizer.

The Water Hyacinth Project (cofunded by the EPA, Solar Energy Research Institute, NASA, University of Florida, University of Arizona, and several other corporations) was a well-publicized experiment in using the otherwise undesirable plant to absorb organic waste in the water through its floating roots. The plants were then harvested for either composting or some sort of animal feed. However, cattle found the stuff unappetizing, and so far the processed hyacinths haven't found an ideal purpose. The program, therefore, has been suspended.

One by-product of the constant search for bigger, better, faster amusements at the park and for bigger, fancier resorts and restaurants, is that the demand for power has mushroomed. (That's not a pun, but in the late 1980s Disney also participated in a simulated nuclear waste disposal project that was federally funded. No real "hot" waste was burned, and Disney said it agreed to help only to get rid of more ordinary garbage. But that didn't turn out to be very cost-efficient either. However, the experiment did reveal that the state charter theoretically permits Disney to own and operate a nuclear fission reactor.) The amount of power needed to run the whole park when it opened would barely maintain the Magic Kingdom today.

Walt Disney World produces approximately one-quarter of its own energy through a combination of electric generation, energy recycling, and solar energy; the rest is purchased from outside sources. The Central Energy Plant produces about 30% of the electricity, all of the hot water, and most of the air conditioning water used in the park. It uses both gas turbine and steam turbine techniques to drive generators that can run on either diesel fuel or natural gas, whichever is less expensive at any particular time. (Disney had previously experimented with blast-furnace incineration using solid waste to produce steam heat, but it wasn't cost-efficient.) The steam from the turbines is then recaptured and recycled for use in heating water, running the air conditioning system, and so on.

A secondary facility at Epcot provides chilled and warm water for that park. The newer office buildings have some solar panels, and most of the later resorts have been designed using such energy-conserving techniques as angling windows, natural shade, and ventilation. Power is further conserved by computers that monitor high- and low-use cycles at the park.

Even so, power is not always available on demand, especially in Florida. So what happens in a regional blackout from a hurricane or other disaster? If you're in Disney World, not much. The company has a diesel generator capable of running all critical systems in the park. And in case the natural gas pipeline is damaged, the park has more than a million gallons of diesel fuel on-hand.

Mickey & Company

The Cast and Crew

What's it like to work in Wonderland? It seems to depend to a great extent on whether you were hired in the 20th century or in the 21st. Veterans are frequently outspoken on the benefits of the World; in and of itself, the number of employees who stay with the company for 20 and 30 years is a fair recommendation. In fact, the membership of Disneyana, a combination fan club/convention/souvenir collectors' army that convenes twice a year, includes as many current and former employees as plain ol' Mickey fans. The seniors who have made second careers or spend their semi-retirement there, as it can seem, are also strong boosters.

The explanation seems to be that the company instills the crew with both a sense of responsibility and a sense of fun, albeit a somewhat directed one. Every new employee, or cast member as they are always called (even in those nonperforming departments of the company), is required to take a two-day course called "Traditions": a mix of company legend, behavioral guidelines, and psychosocial bonding. "You come out totally believing in 'The Disney Way'," said a five-year veteran. "It's almost like Walt is alive and well. It's a total immersion thing. You talk about 'Disney this' and 'Disney that': We call it getting dosed with pixie dust. It lasts about a year—and of course some people have to go through it again."

Employees also have benefits with emotionally, if not economically, addictive properties: All full-time employees get at least 12 days' free admission to the parks a year, plus free parking and access to all other World facilities, including a cast-only recreation park. Salaried employees have "silver passes," good for unlimited free access for four people. (Corporate execs carry "gold passes," good for as many people as they want to bring in.)

"This is the greatest job," said Mark Mattern, who was then head of the Disney Institute's culinary school; he's now with a private media relations firm. "You get to teach people hands-on, you have state-of-the-art facilities, medical insurance, a great place to live—and I can take my kid to the Magic Kingdom any time I want." And the pay, at least according to Mattern, is competitive; Mattern said he was offered the job of host chef for the Atlanta Olympics but turned it down for the Disney World job.

There are frequent organized cast functions and special events such as "Thursday night at the movies." And whenever there are new amusements or rides about to open, it's the cast members who get to play guinea pig. One woman remembered riding Splash Mountain so many times that she knew all the songs by heart—"and they kept yelling over the PA, 'Please keep your hands in the boat!' because there was a huge splash fight going on."

"Yeah, you get a little jaded working here sometimes, until you're out with somebody who's never seen the park before," agreed another cast member. "And then they go nuts and all of a sudden you think, 'Hey, I work at this place that really makes people happy!'"

On the other hand, the last several classes of college interns and the younger seasonal employees—i.e., those with little seniority—have reported less magical experiences. Partly it was the fault of the famous loss of civility among Americans that has made even Disney visitors pushy and impatient (reducing cast members to tears on occasion). "The foreigners were much more polite," says one former employee. "You could definitely tell who the Americans were." The trend also reflected staff cutbacks and haphazard transfers employees with less experience in management positions.

Often, the decreased morale was caused by a combination of these factors. One college intern, who had been assured she would be working in media relations in ways that would benefit her broadcast journalism major, wound up working in costume sales at Disney-MGM Studios. She was annoyed not only by the rudeness of guests—including one who threw a costume in her face when she couldn't find the size he wanted—but also with inept supervisors who replaced her original managers part-way through the summer.

Not only that, but staff cutback (and erratic post-9/11 atten-dance) meant that some college interns worked 10 to 12 hours a day at hot dog and popcorn wagons.

"For $6 [an hour], I could have stayed home this summer and made a lot more money," said one disaffected cast member. "Plus we had to pay a ridiculous amount of rent,"—$1,600 a month for six interns in a three-bedroom Disney apartment.

"Pixie Dust"

If all those Japanese-style training manuals had been published 40 years ago, you'd think Disney had read them. When it comes to in-house behavior, Disney has little interest in self-expression. The training phases of Disney employment are just as exhaus-tively detailed as the planning, zoning, paint colors, and wallpa-per at the castle.

In fact, "Traditions" is being exported to outside companies, just as some management groups invited Japanese executives in during the 1980s. *(In Search of Excellence* author, Tom Peters, cited "Traditions" as one of the best such indoctrination pro-grams in 1982.)* The Disney University has turned some Disney Way rules into a shakedown seminar for managers that, for example, persuaded one public hospital to set up a "back stage" for the staff, where they could relax from the stress of emer-gency treatment and even death. Others package management skills. Another group of professional development courses are designed specifically for educators, to show them ways of adapt-ing marketing and motivation techniques to the classroom.

These professional services are being aggressively promoted at a time when many corporations are thinning out exactly the middle-level managers who might have run such programs. Among graduating "classes" of the university have been employ-ees of the CIA, Burger King and McDonald's, and Coke and Pepsi. The three-day programs cost about $2,000 per person, and mini-seminars are available for business conventions and special meetings.

The business and technical training at Walt Disney World has become so proficient that college students can work on-site for credits in business, food and beverage management, human resources, retailing, and so on. More than 3,000 13-week interns take part in this hands-on training every year. (In typical pixie dust style, graduates can earn either "Mouster's" or "Ducktorate" degrees.) There are also full-term internships available through the corporations that sponsor the various pavilions.

Working at Disney World does not suit everybody. One man who got a summer job as a character role was busted almost immediately for improvising and was exiled to an ice cream stand. "I was just part of a machine that operated exactly the same way, paraded at exactly the same time, orchestrated by other machines . . . and all for minimum wage." He stayed only a few weeks.

Another suggested that the company had become too large to provide a "personalized" experience. "I took the communications course, and one of our speeches had to be about the corporation and how it developed. I had no idea how much stuff they own—they have their hands in everything!"

But the company is very up-front about its requirements. In the first rather sketchy interview, prospective employees are told about the dress code, the likelihood that they'll be working on holidays, which are especially busy park days, and so on. Only if they accept these basic requirements are they scheduled for in-depth interviews. Those who will be in contact with the public are interviewed in small groups so that they have to interact; craft workers are evaluated one-on-one by their professional peers.

With rare exceptions, the rules have remained unchanged for 40 years, since the opening of Disneyland: no ad-libbing, no fraternizing, no obvious makeup, except in character. Cast members, costumed or not, are required to look as squeaky-clean as the original Mouseketeers (and with haircuts for men almost as short as Spin and Marty's). Women who color their hair must look completely "natural": One new summer recruit was sent home to get red of her fairly unobtrusive blonde highlights; but when she returned with re-dyed hair, she was told it was too dark and no longer matched her complexion. Men are now allowed to sport well-trimmed mustaches and ½-inch side-burns, but no stylishly pointed 'burns, goatees, beards, or—at the other extreme—no shaved or patterned heads. Otherwise, the rules also say no visible tattoos; no nose or other piercing except for the ear lobe, and only two earring holes—and only for women; no obvious bralessness; no bright nail polish or excessively long nails; and no excess jewelry.

Those cast members chosen to portray the cartoon characters such as Mickey and Minnie, called "greeters" because they interact with the public, must never speak. (Any Mouse-loving kid would immediately know it was the "wrong" voice.) Those who do speak must stick to the script; improvisation is allowed in only very specific situations. Certain characters, senior positions, so to speak, are encouraged to ad-lib a little: usually cruise captains, train conductors, and so on. It would be hard to stop some of them: Among the alumni pilots of the famously pun-filled Jungle Cruise are Robin Williams, Steve Martin, and Michael J. Fox. Even the professionals and adult education instructors, who work face-to-face with visitors, still find their new, looser public relations rules confusing: "I never thought in 25 years I'd be talking with a guest, much less out drinking with her."

It's against the rules to be seen wearing your costume anywhere but in your assigned area, so all cast members must begin and end every shift by changing clothes. Because no one is allowed to wear the costumes home or to sleep on park grounds, employees who have a late shift followed by an early one may find their off hours quite abbreviated. (In a cost-cutting move, cast members have been asked to launder whatever of their own costumes they can—a potential savings of $1 million a year, according to CFO Thomas Staggs.) Many of the costumes are heavy and hot, and some that have limited vision and restricted movements can be painful and even hazardous. Characters say that a surprising number of children, and even some adults, want to punch or kick them or trip them. Some female fantasy characters, such as Snow White, are occasionally victims of fondling.

Even behind the scenes, few things are as they seem. Considering the costume requirements, many of the cast members chosen for most "greeter" parts have to be fairly small. "They're just very little people," said a taller co-worker. "And Mickey's actually a girl—which gets weird when she starts kissing people."

There is one other fantastic quality of Walt Disney World, and you may not have noticed it yet: nobody is allowed to die here. This is a lesson cast members have to learn early on. Of course, it's a matter of perception, not reality: with hundreds of thousands of visitors every day, Disney World's daily population is larger than many cities in the country, and sheer statistical probability means that every once in a while a guest will pass into the great Adventureland. But not onstage—not if the cast members can help it. Employees tell very hushed stories about having to pass off corpses as drunks or victims of ordinary trippings. In a fairly notorious case, a man jumped from the top-floor restaurant of the Contemporary Resort into the atrium, and there were shell-shocked staffers mumbling, "He's okay, he'll be fine, just a moment, please." Visitors have drowned—at least one was dismembered when she was pulled under one of the ferries—and so have cast members, including a recent case of a scuba diver who apparently became light-headed, surfaced in some confusion, and hit his head on the underside of the dock, blacking out.

As an employer, Disney has some progressive attitudes, including some that are implicit proof of change. Only a few years ago, a gay couple sued Disney World because they had been prevented from dancing together; these days, the company extends insurance benefits to same-sex partners, for example (at least a tacit acknowledgment that many of its own employees are gay), and gay and lesbian groups have convened at Walt Disney World for a long weekend for several years, partying and parading.

A bus driver described his job as being a model of flexibility: he can work either four 10-hour days or five 8-hour shifts, has regular breaks, and depending on his seniority, could work his way into the shift times he preferred.

Since the mid-1990s, Disney has been an especially visible employer of middle-aged and even senior cast members who are not only reassuring to young children—"grandmotherly"—but who can be particularly candid about rides and conveniences with the rapidly increasing number of older visitors. These older cast members not only enjoy the social interaction, but in many cases, they rely on the additional income and access to group benefits.

Post-9/11, Disney has also sought out retired law enforcement officers (though admittedly often from such relatively nonthreatening positions as toll both police and private security patrols) to work in park security. However, other cast members are skeptical of these "guards," as they reputedly receive only minimal training. One cast member carrying his own security radio recalls hearing a request for a security officer's presence at the Wilderness Lodge, only to then hear a supervisor advise that that "there is no security officer at Wilderness." And it has become a sort of game, particularly among groups of impatient teens, to circumvent the bag-inspection lines by distracting and slipping past the guards.

Walt Disney World also has some very corporate attitudes. It is the region's, and the state's, largest employer, even when it isn't in the midst of major construction. In relatively quiet times, it employs 50,000 people full-time and about 8,000 part-time—not just the 200 or so Mickeys and Cinderellas but the guides at the rides, street sweepers, animal-care specialists, food and beverage workers, camera technicians, computer programmers, agriculturalists, lifeguards, makeup artists, the maintenance workers who paint the Carrousel every night, and the ones who sew up ripped costumes every day.

But that also means increased labor costs, and a couple of years ago, faced with billion-dollar labor costs, the company decided that employees should share the expense of health care premiums that had always been free. Management also decided to try to use more part-time workers, who are not covered by contracts, reduce benefits for full-time employees, and hire outside contractors more frequently.

The renegotiations were drawn-out and often quite acrimonious. Eventually the unions ratified a package of five health-care plans and 3–4% raises. It also required that those employees who were replaced by contract labor be found full-time jobs within the company.

In 1998, another lengthy series of contract negotiations began, but only about 40% of the company's service employees had bothered to join any of the six possible unions—and only a third of those voted on the proposals. So Disney, with a surplus of possible recruits (Florida's unemployment rate is almost nil), continues to play Stingy—the Eighth Dwarf. Remember, Disney also owns ABC and had no hesitation about locking out

2,400 NABET members after they expressed impatience with a two-year contract dispute by staging a one-day walkout.

The atmosphere has been a little more tense since the events of September 11th. During the general slowdown of 2001, cast members were laid off or retired without being replaced. The government-ordered corporate course in sexual harassment was used by some cast members, according to inside sources, as a way of either sandbagging rivals or promoting one's own career.

But despite the long impasses, the pixie dust seems to stick. Except for a few "street-theater" demonstrations against the company, the esprit de corps remains unusually high. A character actor, who had complained at humorous length about the weight of his costume on a hot day, wound up saying, "But it sure beats sitting at a desk all day."

Even cast members who have had bad experiences tend to find ways to excuse the corporation. Two women chefs, who said they'd been looked down on or ridiculed in the kitchens, attributed the bias to the culinary culture rather than the Disney Way. "I can't say we didn't have problems getting positions of power, but that's the usual problem of being a girl in a kitchen full of boys. Only a few executive chefs are women." (Disney tries to make it look better, perhaps, by making their few women, including the sushi chef at the California Grill and executive chef Anette Grecchi of Narcoosee's, especially visible.)

As one woman who has been employed by and quit the company several times said, "I still love the place. I hope to go back. For all its problems, I still feel a great deal of loyalty to it, and I wouldn't like to see a bad book written about it."

As mentioned in "The Mouse That Scored," everybody, even CEO Michael Eisner, is on a first-name basis. Even official nametags are printed only with first names. (And those, according to recent offers, are worth at least $25 on the Disneyana black market.) "After eight years, I can go anywhere on the property and know somebody. Of course, I may only know his first name," a cast member joked.

Disney prefers to hire from within for management positions, because they can be sure that the employees understand the operation and support it. Opportunities to move up, or just into different areas of the corporation, are posted in the cast center and circulated through in-house newsletters. (Applicants are reinterviewed, retrained, and sometimes re-"dusted" as well.) Younger employees are often reminded that there are many executives in the company who started out at very menial levels—most famously Dick Nunis, the onetime Disneyland dishwasher, who was head of operations during the construction of Walt Disney World and wound up being president of both U.S. amusement parks. Eisner himself started out as a page, although at NBC.

The stories are a little misleading, perhaps. Nunis, for example, though he is still a corporate vice-president, was eased out of real power some years ago. A highly placed Orlando businessman says that Eisner realized that Nunis' sometimes truculent style was not improving Disney's public image. Fewer managers who have fallen short of expectations are given second chances in other departments, which was standard procedure in the old days. And with the increased emphasis on public access in the park and on showing off the serious science and conservation efforts being made, a greater number of staffers with traditional credentials are needed.

Still, cast members say they are constantly encouraged to look into management openings as well as on- or off-stage jobs. Periodic evaluations of staff prospects allow supervisors to maintain a sense of their employees' hopes and their likely professional fit; employees who don't do well in one area are given second chances in other departments. The Disney Company has unusually low employee turnover.

The foreign pavilions at Epcot's World Showcase, and even a few of the exotic attractions elsewhere, require foreign cast members. Consequently, the company has set up a "World College" extension program that recruits international cast members and gets them cultural exchange visas for one year. But Disney takes its responsibility as "host family" very seriously. The exchange students are the only cast members who actually live on campus, in a community called Vista Way that is run as strictly as an old-style college dorm—strict security check-ins and no mixed-sex apartment mates. The major problem the World College has, cast members say, is that none of the students ever want to go home at year's end.

Uncle Scrooge

Remember that not all Disney features were commercial successes the first time around. Remember also that animation was still an unformed creature, shedding its skin, growing feathers—and that it was a brainstorm of Walt's to withdraw the features from circulation and only periodically (every seven years—just long enough to develop a new audience) to re-release them.

The fact remains that a surprising number of the live actors who gave voice (or music) to some of the biggest cartoon hits in the Disney stable had to sue the company to get their fair share of the proceeds. And as with its labor negotiations, Disney seems willing to risk losing face by taking on some of the best-known faces, or voices, in the business.

One less attractive aspect of Disney corporate behavior is its occasional tone of "it's not personal, it's business." Even, sometimes, when it comes to old friends. The Philadelphia Orchestra, which not only provided the background music but whose members actually appeared with maestro Leopold Stokowski in the first segments of *Fantasia,* sued for royalties when the video was released; Disney settled.

Peggy Lee, who cowrote and sang a half-dozen songs for the 1955 *Lady and the Tramp,* sued for what she said was $10 million in unpaid video royalties; a jury awarded her about a third of what she asked. Mary Losta, the voice of Sleeping Beauty, and Ilene Woods Shaunessey, the voice of Cinderella, have followed suit. There was a long struggle with Jim Henson over a licensing agreement that Disney said allowed it to put a Muppets show into Disney-MGM Studios; the suits and countersuits became quite acrimonious before they were settled. (Ironically, Disney-MGM Studios' chairman Jeffrey Katzenberg, who later filed suit against the Disney Company himself, had frowned on the Henson-Disney battle, telling reporters that in fighting so many lawsuits, the Disney Company "ran the risk of creating the impression that Disney has become a lot less friendly.")

One of the most puzzling cases involved former cast member Daryan Faerve, who in 1987 suggested the company package little tubes of "pixie dust"—in this case, colored sparkling dust—as souvenirs. Faerve was told, in effect, thanks but no thanks. Four months later, Disney itself began marketing just such a souvenir.

Since Faerve had obtained state and federal trademark protection, he eventually settled with the company for $100,000. But as one slightly embarrassed cast member commented, "It's amazing they hadn't already thought of it—but it's even worse they tried to screw their own guy."

Disney has also been accused of taking itself and its trademarks far too seriously. It once ordered the removal of a Disney character from the side of a garbage truck because the image it conveyed apparently wasn't elevated enough. In 1989 it forced a preschool center to paint over a mural of Disney characters. (Universal promptly offered to paint a new Flintstones mural for free.) The same year, the Disney Company threatened to sue the Academy of Movie Arts and Sciences because a skit on the annual Oscars telecast featured Tom Cruise dancing with Snow White, an engagement Disney apparently felt might damage her, well, snow-white reputation. Only after the Academy formally apologized did Disney withdraw, although by then the whole situation had been chewed over by dozens of comics and commentators.

In 1991, the company that owns the merchandising rights to Winnie the Pooh claimed Disney was cheating it out of millions of dollars in royalty payments. The suit has still not been settled; amazingly, the increasingly complex case and its various offshoots have been conducted in nearly complete secrecy. However, it was revealed that in 2001, Disney was fined $90,000 for destroying documents that might have been relevant to the case. More disturbingly, the journalist who broke the penalty story, Nikki Finke, was fired by the *New York Post* only a few weeks after her story ran—reportedly, after Disney executives pressured the paper's editors. Michael Eisner was rumored to have complained directly to sometime business partner and *Post* owner Rupert Murdoch about Finke's stories.

Then there are the difficulties with cast members who take advantage of Disney rather than the other way around. Even back in 1996, a one-day adult pass to the Magic Kingdom, Epcot, or Disney-MGM Studios cost a little over $40; a four-day pass for one day in each park, plus a "wild card," was about $135; and a four-day pass good for any park, any time, cost about $200. Other big tickets include length-of-stay passes (about $300 for ten days), annual passes ($250 for the three theme parks, with a yearly $225 renewal), and World-wide annual passes that include the water parks and Pleasure Island (nearly $350, with a $300 renewal fee).

Obviously, park passes are big moneymakers, which makes them tempting targets for thieves and counterfeiters—some of whom are cast members. In 1994, a Disney employee took $1.75 million worth of tickets from a company vault and sold them for $200,000. The Disney employee was caught, but his accomplice was not. Net loss: a million and a half. In 1988, another employee just stuffed his pockets with tickets and took them home. He was caught and ordered to pay $58,000, but that was only a little more than half the estimated value of the tickets. And in 1993, three workers at Disney-MGM Studios worked out a ticket-upgrade scam that cost the company more than $400,000.

Afterword

"Mirror, Mirror, on the Wall . . ."

In the forests of eastern Volusia County, not far from where Walt Disney's parents were married, there is a nearly full-scale replica of the cottage in which Snow White lived with the Seven Dwarfs. Built along Spruce Creek and using original celluloids as carpenter's blueprints (with only these two-dimensional guidelines, the builder had to see the movie several times and then eye the proportions), it was the dream cottage of an old friend of Disney's named Judge Alfred Nippert, the son-in-law of soap magnate James Gamble. It was built in 1938, the year after *Snow White* was released and nearly two decades before the opening of Disneyland. When Walt himself toured it, he was so touched that he sent the man full-sized dolls of Snow White and all seven friends.

The princess lay in a glass coffin in the living room. The fireplace mantel was whole timber; the heavy Gothic doors had iron-strap hinges; and original cells from the movie hung around the walls. It was a perfect Black Forest fantasy, except that most of the wood was Florida cypress. Outside were lavish gardens with stone walkways, a witch's hut, a mine shaft, a wishing well, a rock garden, a garden pool built of fieldstone with a lion's head fountain, "stalagmites" of cypress knees, and statues of dwarfs and animals. It was open for tours into the 1950s, when it fell into disrepair. It was rediscovered and restored a few years ago using historic photographs and is now part of the Gamble Place history and education center operated by the Daytona Beach Museum of Arts and Sciences.

There are photos of the judge, pipe in hand, rocking in one of the cypress chairs he had built for the place. It's almost irresistible to imagine that he retreated to the cottage as a refuge from the intricacies of judicial rhetoric—that he longed for a world in which good and evil were so clearly opposed, and the latter so totally vanquished. But even more, it's sweet to think that such an august professional knew, with as much affection as any small child, the names of those magnificent seven: Sneezy, Sleepy, Happy, Dopey, Grumpy, Bashful, and Doc.

When astronaut Sally Ride was asked to describe her journey into space, she called it "an E-ticket ride." In the early days, Disneyland and Disney World both used an ornate system of ticket books. "A" tickets were for "A" rides, "B" tickets for "B" attractions, and so on. The most elaborate attractions required the expensive "E" tickets, so Sally Ride was really saying the launch had lived up to her wildest childhood fantasies.

How many of us can honestly say we have never been touched by Walt Disney's dream? wouldn't love to fly, stay young forever, slay the dragon, or become a real live person? Maybe that's what still makes Walt Disney World fascinating—not its technological wizardry, but the simple wonder at its heart. Overshadowed though the Magic Kingdom may be by the newer attractions, it remains Walt's real World, and his great gift to us. Maybe it is only an imitation paradise, but if we don't have models to go by, how will we remember—in this exhausting, selfish, violent, and often soul-crushing world—that there was ever a star to wish on? If a child does not say, "I believe, I do believe," how much darker and narrower will his future be? If she does not learn to love A Bear of Very Little Brain, how will she learn to hear the inarticulate sufferers of the world?

I believe in the power of imagination. I believe in the unexplored possibilities of the spirit. And I believe that the heart, like any other muscle, grows stiff if it is not exercised regularly.

I believe.

Appendix

A Brief History of the World

1961

Encouraged by the phenomenal success of Disneyland in Anaheim, California, Walt Disney envisions a second theme park located somewhere in the eastern United States.

1962

As Disney formulates plans for his eastern park, he focuses on four essential prerequisites:

1. The park must be located in a temperate climate that allows year-round operation.
2. Enough land must be acquired to insulate the park from the sort of crass commercialism and conflicting environment that enveloped Disneyland.
3. Disney must have absolute autonomy and authority in the development of the new property and must be essentially exempt from development covenants, building codes, and other local restrictions.
4. State and county government must commit to providing necessary infrastructure (highways, etc.) to support the Disney project.

1963

Because of its weather and commitment to tourism, Florida is selected as the best location for the new park.

The search bypasses coastal areas to focus on the Orlando area, where large expanses of land are available at bargain prices. Orlando is also situated at the crossroads of Florida's primary traffic arteries.

The concept for the new park first expands to become a complete destination resort and then subsequently enlarges to become Epcot, the Experimental Prototype Community of Tomorrow. According to Walt Disney's vision, the entire development known as Epcot would contain a Disneyland clone theme park, hotels, lakes, highways, recreation areas, and a futuristic utopian city populated initially by Disney employees.

Negotiations begin with the State of Florida for tax concessions, local jurisdictional waivers, and infrastructure commitments.

1964

Using a number of agents, Disney clandestinely begins acquiring land. Ultimately, almost 28,000 acres are acquired from more than 100 property owners at an average cost of about $200 per acre.

1965

Though the project is first exposed by the *Orlando Sentinel,* the official announcement is made on November 16, at a press conference with Walt Disney, his brother Roy Disney, and Florida Governor Hayden Burns. Walt Disney shares his expectation that the vacation destination would evolve to become a utopian community offering a way of life that marries the values of turn-of-the-century America with the technology of the future.

1966

Detailed planning of the Florida Disney project continues until the death of Walt Disney on December 15.

1967

After Walt's death, Roy Disney, Donn B. Tatum, and E. Cardon Walker, the company's top executives, carry the project forward, but begin to diverge from Walt's vision. Site preparation begins. Swamps and wetlands are reclaimed through the development of a system of water-control channels.

1968

Legislation is passed creating the Reedy Creek Development District, a veritable state within a state. The legislation allows Disney to develop its 28,000 acres without interference from Orange and Osceola counties.

1969

Construction begins on "Phase I," to include the Magic Kingdom, the Contemporary Resort, the Polynesian Resort, Fort Wilderness Campground, two 18-hole golf courses, and the Disney Transportation System. The target date for the opening is October 1, 1971.

1970

Construction continues, including the creation of the Seven Seas Lagoon, a 200-acre lake fronting the Magic Kingdom that connects to Bay Lake by canal.

1971

Construction clips along at a frantic pace as the opening date approaches. Before the gates open, the project will have involved approximately 9,000 workers and cost $400 million.

During all of September, while finishing touches are applied, more than 100,000 Disney employees and local guests preview the project.

On October 1, Walt Disney World opens to the public. The William Windsor family is the first to enter.

A gala grand opening is staged October 23–25, with Arthur Fiedler conducting the World Symphony Orchestra. The Magic Kingdom's opening parade features a 1,076-piece marching band with 76 trombones à la the *Music Man.*

Circle-Vision 360's *America the Beautiful* opens in November, followed by *Flight to the Moon* in December.

The attendance record for 1971 is set on December 29, when 69,500 guests tour the Magic Kingdom.

1972

If You Had Wings opens in Tomorrowland.

Six additional monorail trains and two ferry boats are brought on line.

Attendance totals just under 11 million guests for the first complete year of operation (almost exactly the same first-year total registered by Euro Disneyland 20 years later).

72,000-plus guests visit the Magic Kingdom on December 27, setting a new one-day record.

1973

The Golf Resort Hotel (later called the Disney Inn) opens. The quietest and most adult of all Disney lodging properties, the hotel was leased to the Department of Defense and renamed Shades of Green in 1994.

Pirates of the Caribbean opens in New Orleans Square.

The *Walt Disney Story* premiers on Main Street.

The Swan Boats open on the drawbridge side of Cinderella Castle.

Tom Sawyer Island begins operations in Frontierland.

The Richard F. Irvine Steamboat is launched in Liberty Square.

Another one-day attendance record is set on April 17, when over 73,000 guests visit the park.

Walt Disney Productions celebrates its 50th anniversary.

Richard Nixon is a guest at the Contemporary Resort.

Construction gets underway on Space Mountain in Tomorrowland.

1974

StarJets begins service in Tomorrowland.

Discovery Island, a bird sanctuary in Bay Lake, opens to the public.

At the Fort Wilderness Campground, the Pioneer Hall dinner theater opens.

Donald Duck turns 40.

On December 27, 74,597 guests pass through the Magic Kingdom turnstiles, setting a new one-day attendance record.

1975

Space Mountain opens in January.

Also in Tomorrowland, the GE *Carousel of Progress* begins its long tenure at Walt Disney World. The attraction had originally been designed by Disney for the 1964 New York World's Fair.

The WEDway PeopleMover comes on line in Tomorrowland.

An updated *America the Beautiful* premiers at Circle-Vision 360.

Mission to Mars replaces Flight to the Moon.

The Lake Buena Vista Shopping Village (later the Walt Disney World Village Marketplace) opens in March.

Plans for Epcot are revealed and differ significantly from Walt Disney's original concept.

Two single-day attendance records are set at the Magic Kingdom: 82,300 guests on March 25 and then 82,400 guests on New Year's Eve.

1976

The River Country water park opens adjacent to the Fort Wilderness Campground.

The Magic Kingdom welcomes its 50-millionth visitor in March.

1977

The *Empress Lilly* Riverboat restaurant (named for Walt Disney's wife) is dedicated at the Lake Buena Vista Shopping Village.

The Main Street Electrical Parade premiers at the Magic Kingdom.

A new one-day attendance record is set on December 28, as almost 83,000 guests tour the Magic Kingdom.

1978

Mickey Mouse celebrates his 50th birthday.

Opening for Epcot is targeted for 1982.

One-day attendance breaks the 85,000-guest threshold on March 28.

1979

Construction begins on Big Thunder Mountain Railroad.

Construction begins on Epcot Center.

The Magic Kingdom receives its 100-millionth visitor on October 22, almost eight years exactly from the date of the park's grand opening.

1980

Big Thunder Mountain Railroad opens in Frontierland.

The old single-day attendance record is shattered when 93,000 guests inundate the Magic Kingdom on New Year's Eve.

Construction continues on Epcot Center and on a new monorail loop connecting the Transportation and Ticket Center to Epcot Center.

1981

Broadway at the Top dinner show opens at the Top of the World restaurant at the Contemporary Resort.

Construction continues at Epcot Center.

1982

Epcot Center opens to the public on October 1. Completely transformed by corporate Disney, Epcot Center is a theme park as opposed to the working, prototypical community that Walt Disney envisioned.

The grand opening was covered by over 1,000 print and broadcast journalists.

1983

Walt Disney World's 150-millionth visitor arrives on April 11.

New World Fantasy, a fireworks, fountains, and laser precursor to *IllumiNations,* debuts on the World Showcase Lagoon at Epcot Center.

1984

Donald Duck celebrates his 50th birthday.

The Moroccan pavilion opens in the World Showcase section of Epcot Center.

A new movie, *American Journeys,* debuts at Circle-Vision 360 in Tomorrowland.

The Big Thunder Shooting Gallery opens in Frontierland.

1985

Responding to an earlier announcement by Universal Studios, Disney unveils plans for the Disney-MGM Studios Tour.

At the Magic Kingdom, Tinkerbell's Flight is added to the Fantasy in the Sky fireworks spectacular.

A daytime show featuring airplanes, kites, and speedboats premiers on the World Showcase Lagoon at Epcot Center.

1986

The Living Seas opens in the Future World section of Epcot Center.

Captain EO replaces *Magic Journeys* at the Magic Eye Theater at the Journey into Imagination pavilion at Epcot Center. *Magic Journeys* reappears in the Magic Kingdom.

Construction gets underway for the Disney-MGM Studios, the Grand Floridian Beach Resort, the Norway pavilion at Epcot Center, and Pleasure Island, a nightlife entertainment complex.

1987

Walt Disney World's 250-millionth visitor arrives. Attendance at Walt Disney World passes the official population of the United States.

In Disney's version of an Elvis impersonator convention, all of the cast members who played Snow White during the Magic Kingdom's first 15 years gathered for a reunion.

The Disney Information Center off I-75 in Ocala opens.

With the introduction of Disney Dollars, Disney begins printing and issuing its own currency.

1988

IllumiNations debuts.

Construction begins on the Wonders of Life pavilion at Epcot Center.

Mickey's Birthdayland, the first new land in the Magic Kingdom, opens in celebration of Mickey Mouse's 60th birthday. Attractions include a stop on the Walt Disney World Railroad, Mickey's House, a stage show presentation of a surprise birthday party, and a chance to meet Mickey in his dressing room for photos.

The Norway pavilion at Epcot Center opens, featuring Maelstrom, an indoor boat ride.

The Grand Floridian Resort opens.

The Caribbean Beach Resort brings the first third of its rooms on line.

1989

Disney-MGM Studios opens May 1, almost two years ahead of rival Universal Studios Florida. Attendance at the new park exceeds expectations and requires enlargement of the parking lot.

Typhoon Lagoon, a water theme park featuring slides and a surf pool, opens June 1.

Pleasure Island opens in late June as a gated attraction with six nightclubs.

Disney and Delta Airlines convert *If You Had Wings* (in Tomorrowland) to Dreamflight.

The Wonders of Life pavilion opens in the Future World section of Epcot Center. Feature attractions include Body Wars and Cranium Command.

1990

Star Tours opens at the Disney-MGM Studios.

Honey, I Shrunk the Kids Movie Set Adventure, a children's playground, debuts at the Disney-MGM Studios.

Here Come the Muppets, a stage show featuring the Muppet characters, kicks off a two-year run at the Studios.

Also at the Studios, Disney launches Sorcery in the Sky fireworks.

The Teenage Mutant Ninja Turtles are added to the live entertainment mix at the Studios.

Mickey's Birthdayland at the Magic Kingdom becomes Mickey's Starland. A new character show featuring characters from the Disney cable channel premiers.

The Walt Disney World Swan and the Walt Disney World Dolphin resorts open near Epcot Center.

The International Gateway opens, providing a direct entrance into Epcot Center through the World Showcase section of the park.

Disney Yacht Club Resort and Disney Beach Club Resort open. Both resorts are within walking distance of the new International Gateway to Epcot Center.

1991

Jim Henson's *MuppetVision 3-D* opens at the Disney-MGM Studios.

Sci-Fi Dine-In Theater initiates service at the Studios.

The SpectroMagic parade replaces the Main Street Electrical Parade in the Magic Kingdom.

The Port Orleans Resort opens.

1992

Walt Disney World records its 400-millionth guest.

Splash Mountain opens in Frontierland at the Magic Kingdom.

The Studios launch a new parade based on the Disney animated feature *Aladdin.*

Legend of the Little Mermaid, a theater presentation, debuts at the Disney-MGM Studios.

Disney's Dixie Landings Resort opens in January.

Disney begins selling memberships in the Disney Vacation Club Resort, a time-share development.

The Osprey Ridge and Eagle Pine golf courses open at Disney's Bonnet Creek Golf Club.

1993

The American Adventure in the World Showcase section of Epcot Center is renovated.

In the Magic Kingdom, the *Carousel of Progress* in Tomorrowland is updated. To the consternation of some and the joy of others, the "Now Is the Best Time" theme song is scrapped.

The Hall of Presidents is also made current with the addition of President Bill Clinton.

Splashtacular and *The Magical World of Barbie* (the doll) are added to the live entertainment schedule at Epcot Center.

The Walt Disney Story on Main Street is closed. Go figure.

1994

Mary Smith of Decatur, Illinois, becomes the 1-billionth guest to visit a Disney theme park.

Epcot Center changes its name to Epcot '94. Later the "94" is dropped.

The Land pavilion in the Future World section of Epcot is renovated. *Kitchen Kaberet* is replaced by *Food Rocks*. The Listen to the Land boat ride is modified and renamed Living With the Land.

Innoventions, a corporate-sponsored showcase of new products and technologies, replaces Communicore in the Future World section of Epcot.

Honey, I Shrunk the Audience replaces *Captain EO* at the Journey into Imagination pavilion in the Future World section of Epcot.

Spaceship Earth (the attraction in the geodesic sphere) is updated.

Horizons, in the Future World section of Epcot, is closed when no corporate sponsor can be found.

In Tomorrowland at the Magic Kingdom, Mission to Mars closes.

Legend of the Lion King, a stage show, premiers in Fantasyland at the Magic Kingdom.

Also at the Magic Kingdom, Snow White's Adventures is upgraded. Snow White makes an appearance in the attraction for the first time in its 23-year history.

Transportarium, a Circle-Vision 360 attraction designed for EuroDisney, premiers in Tomorrowland at the Magic Kingdom.

The Mickey Mania parade kicks off in the Magic Kingdom.

Sunset Boulevard debuts. A major addition to the Disney-MGM Studios, the Sunset Boulevard area contains attractions, food, and shops.

The Twilight Zone Tower of Terror opens at the Disney-MGM Studios.

The Theater of the Stars is relocated to a more spacious quarters on Sunset Boulevard.

The Back Lot Stage opens, providing the Disney-MGM Studios with another outdoor production venue.

Disney's All-Star Sports Resort opens.

Disney's Wilderness Lodge opens.

Planet Hollywood opens at Pleasure Island.

1995

A total renovation of Tomorrowland in the Magic Kingdom is completed.

Alien Encounter opens in Tomorrowland.

The RocketJets in Tomorrowland are re-themed and called the Astro Orbiter.

The PeopleMover is renamed the Tomorrowland Transit Authority.

In Fantasyland, 20,000 Leagues Under the Sea closes.

Blizzard Beach, the third Disney water park, opens.

The Jazz Club is added to Pleasure Island's nighttime club scene.

Disney's All-Star Music Resort opens.

The Disney Vacation Club changes its name to Disney's Old Key West Resort.

Disney announces plans to build a fourth major theme park, this time with a zoological theme.

1996

The Disney Institute opens, offering a variety of life-enriching educational experiences.

A renovation and expansion of the Walt Disney World Village Marketplace is completed.

Disney's BoardWalk Resort, offering lodging, restaurants, and entertainment, opens opposite the Yacht and Beach Club resorts.

Fantasia Gardens Miniature Golf opens near the Epcot resort hotels.

Disney kicks off Walt Disney World's 25th anniversary party by disguising Cinderella Castle as a huge cake.

Mickey's Starland is converted to Mickey's Toontown Fair. Minnie Mouse's House, Donald Duck's boat, and a mini–roller coaster are added.

Alien Encounter in Tomorrowland is closed, then reopened in a scarier version.

In Future World at Epcot, It's Fun to Be Free, the ride at the World of Motion pavilion, closes to make way for Test Track, a new thrill ride.

Also in Future World, the Universe of Energy is updated.

Disney announces the Village Entertainment District, a 70-acre shopping, restaurant, and nightlife complex to be located near Pleasure Island.

1997

The Coronado Springs resort opens. It surrounds a lagoon and has almost 2,000 rooms.

In November, Downtown Disney opens.

1998

The Animal Kingdom opens in April, except for the Asia section.

The *Fantasmic!* show debuts at Disney-MGM.

Buzz Lightyear's Space Ranger Spin opens at the Magic Kingdom.

The cruise ship *Disney Magic* sets sail in June.

Roy O. Disney is given a star in Hollywood's Walk of Fame.

Cirque de Soleil's *La Nouba* opens at Downtown Disney

1999

Asia opens in the Animal Kingdom.

Test Track opens at Epcot.

Disney's Winter Summerland mini-golf course opens.

The Enchanted Tiki Room show in the Magic Kingdom gets a makeover.

The Many Adventures of Winnie the Pooh opens in the Magic Kingdom.

Rock 'n' Roller Coaster Starring Aerosmith starts rockin' and rollin' at Disney-MGM.

The All-Star Movies Resort opens.

The cruise ship *Disney Wonder* sets sail in August.

The year-long, park-wide Millennium Celebration begins in October, including the addition of a giant, wand-wielding Mickey hand and the "2000" logo to the side of Spaceship Earth in Epcot. The Millennium Village also opens at Epcot, and the *Tapestry of Nations* exhibition and parade begins there as well.

Sounds Dangerous, Bear in the Big Blue House, and *Doug Live!* all open at Disney-MGM.

Lord of the Dance opens at Epcot.

2000

The Villas at Wilderness Lodge open.

2001

The Magic Carpets of Aladdin opens at the Magic Kingdom.

The Animal Kingdom Lodge opens.

Dixie Landings Resort is converted to Port Orleans Riverside, while the original Port Orleans begins transforming into Port Orleans French Quarter.

Who Wants to Be a Millionaire—Play It! opens at Disney-MGM.

In October, the "100 Years of Magic" celebration begins, commemorating Walt Disney's 100th birthday. The related attraction "Walt Disney: One Man's Dream" opens at Disney MGM.

The Disney Institute closes.

2002

Chester and Hester's Dino-Rama! Primeval Whirl opens at Animal Kingdom.

The Beach Club Villas open.

The transformed Port Orleans French Quarter Resort opens.

The half-completed Pop Century resort goes on indefinite hiatus due to the tourism slump.

Index